1 Drawing Vertical Lines

Name

Date

W0038443

To parents
Write your child's name and the date in the boxes
above. Line drawing exercises help your child to
develop basic pencil-control skills. Have your child
draw lines carefully. When your child completes each
exercise, praise him or her.

■ Draw a line from top to bottom connecting the two pictures.

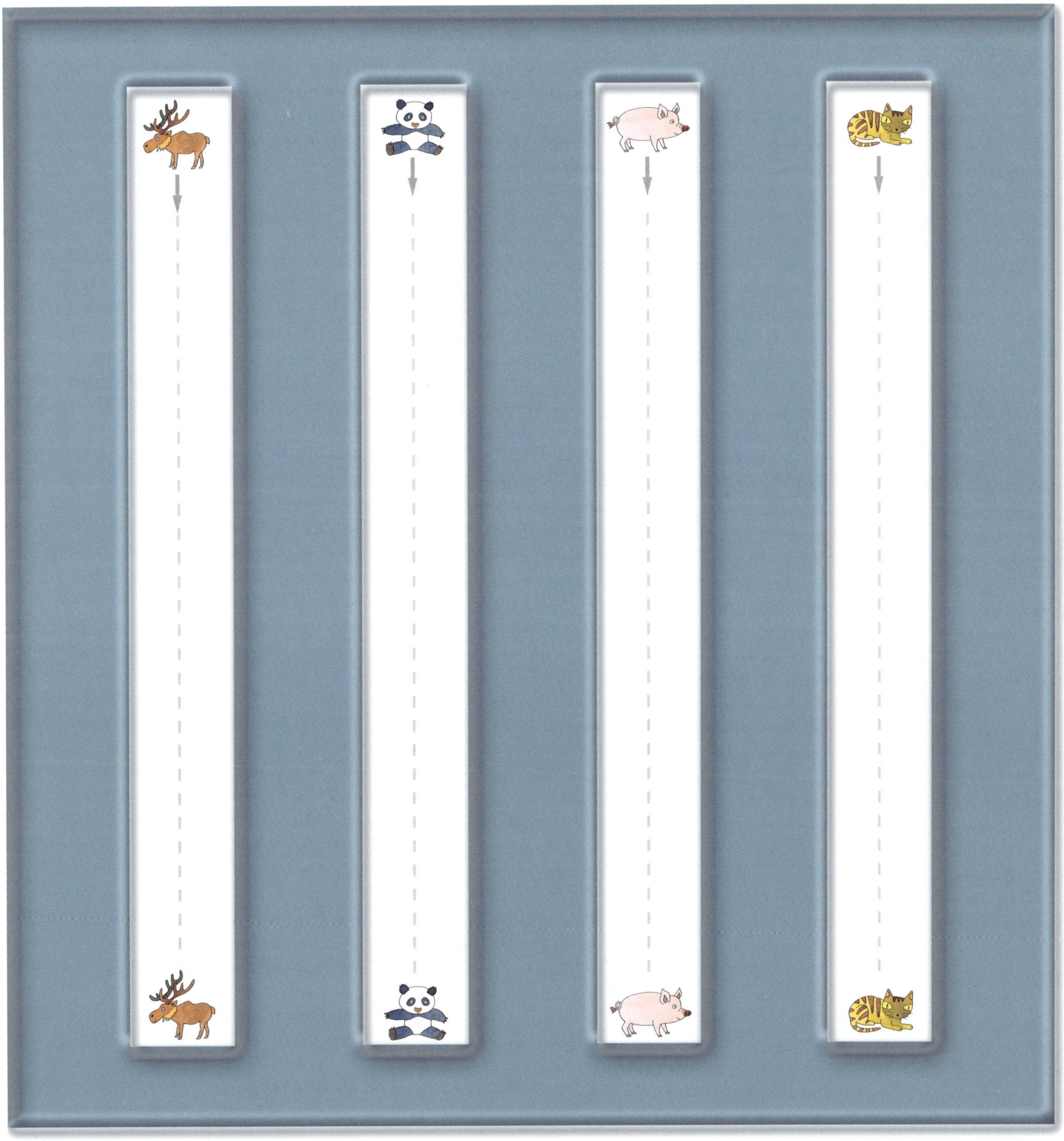

Draw a line from top to bottom connecting the two pictures.

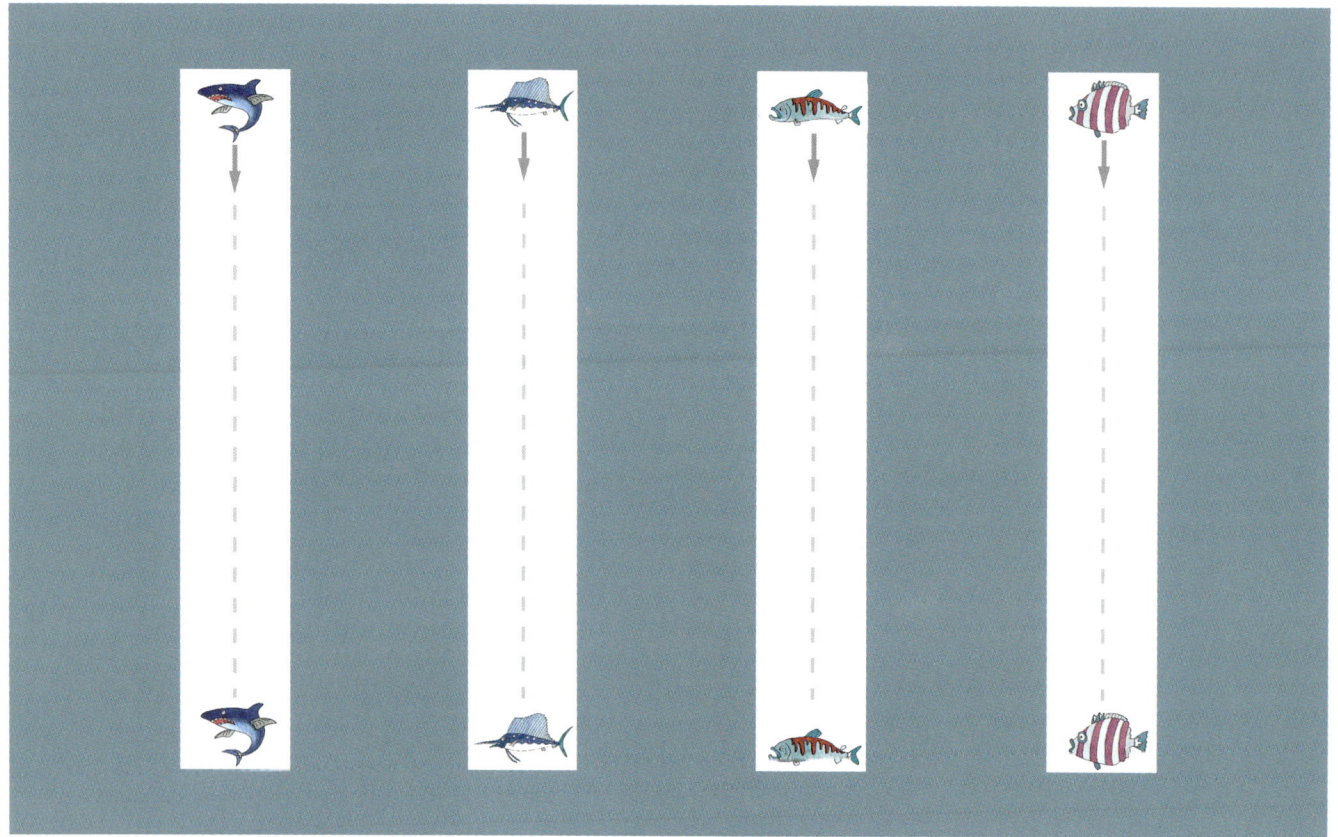

Drawing Horizontal Lines

Name

Date

■ Draw a line from left to right connecting the two pictures.

Draw a line from left to right connecting the two pictures.

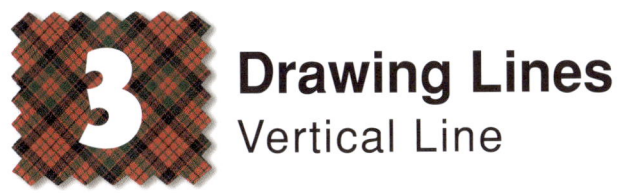

3 Drawing Lines
Vertical Line

Name
Date

■ Draw a line from top to bottom connecting the two pictures.

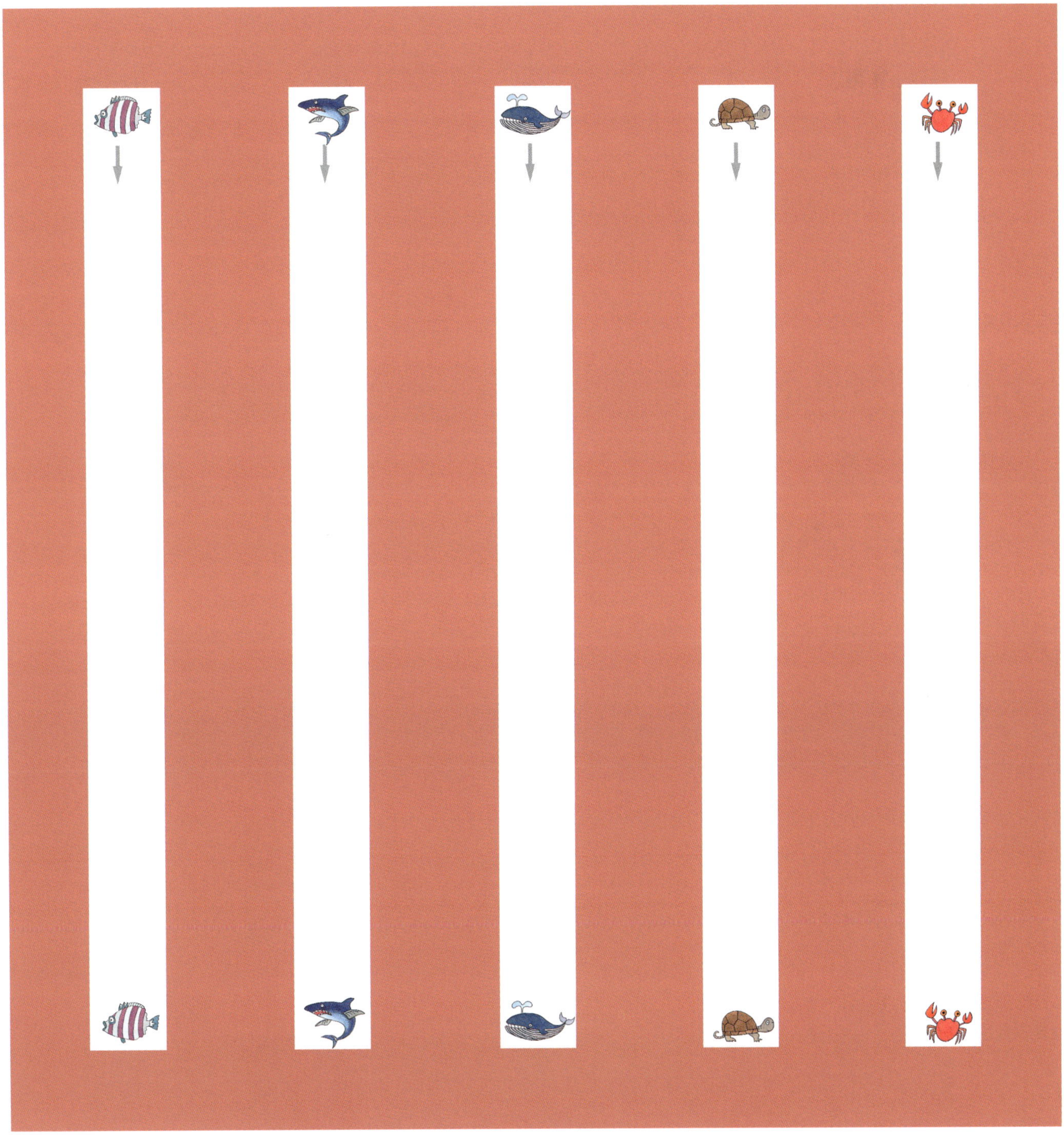

Horizontal Line

■ Draw a line from left to right connecting the two pictures.

Tracing Letters
Writing L

Name

Date

To parents
Before your child begins writing, please read the words on the page and ask your child to repeat the words after you. If your child can recognise the letters, it might be fun to have him or her tell you the name of each letter, and to have your child say the sound of the letter aloud while he or she traces it. If your child is still learning the alphabet, you should tell him or her the name of the letter and teach him or her its sound to say while tracing.

■ Draw a line from the dot (●) to the star (★).

L

LION

| A | B | C | D | E | F | G | H | I | J | K | **L** | M | N | O | P | Q | R | S | T | U | V | W | X | Y | Z |

Writing T

■ Draw a line from the dot (●) to the star (★).
Follow the order of the numbers.

T TOMATO

A B C D E F G H I J K L M N O P Q R S **T** U V W X Y Z

5 Tracing Letters
Writing H

Name

Date

■ Draw a line from the dot (●) to the star (★).
Follow the order of the numbers.

H HAT

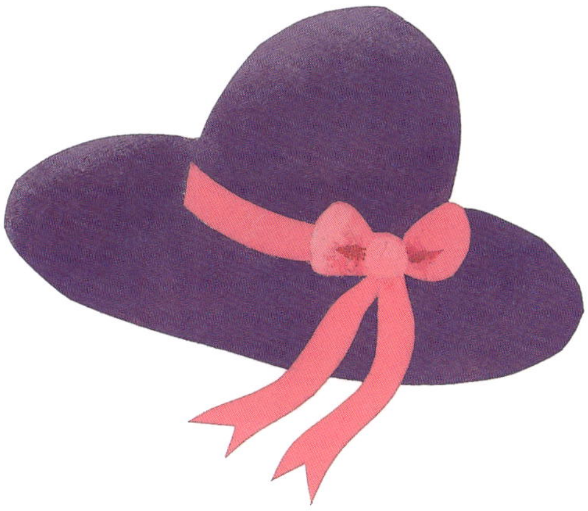

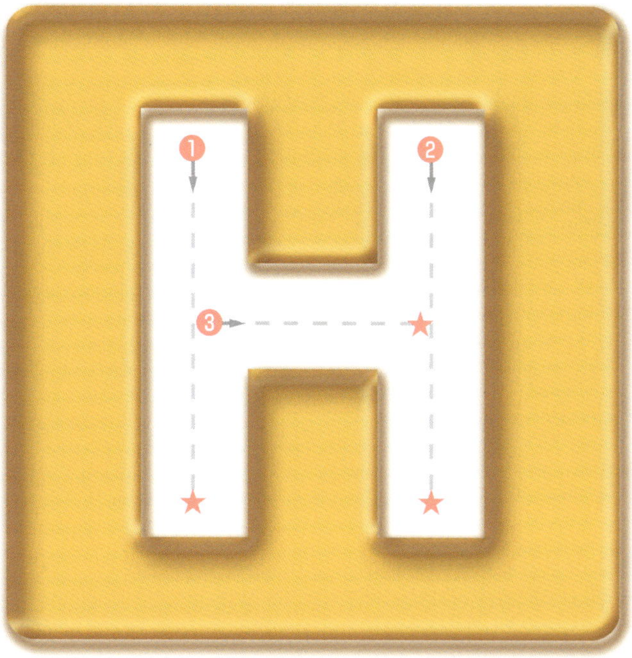

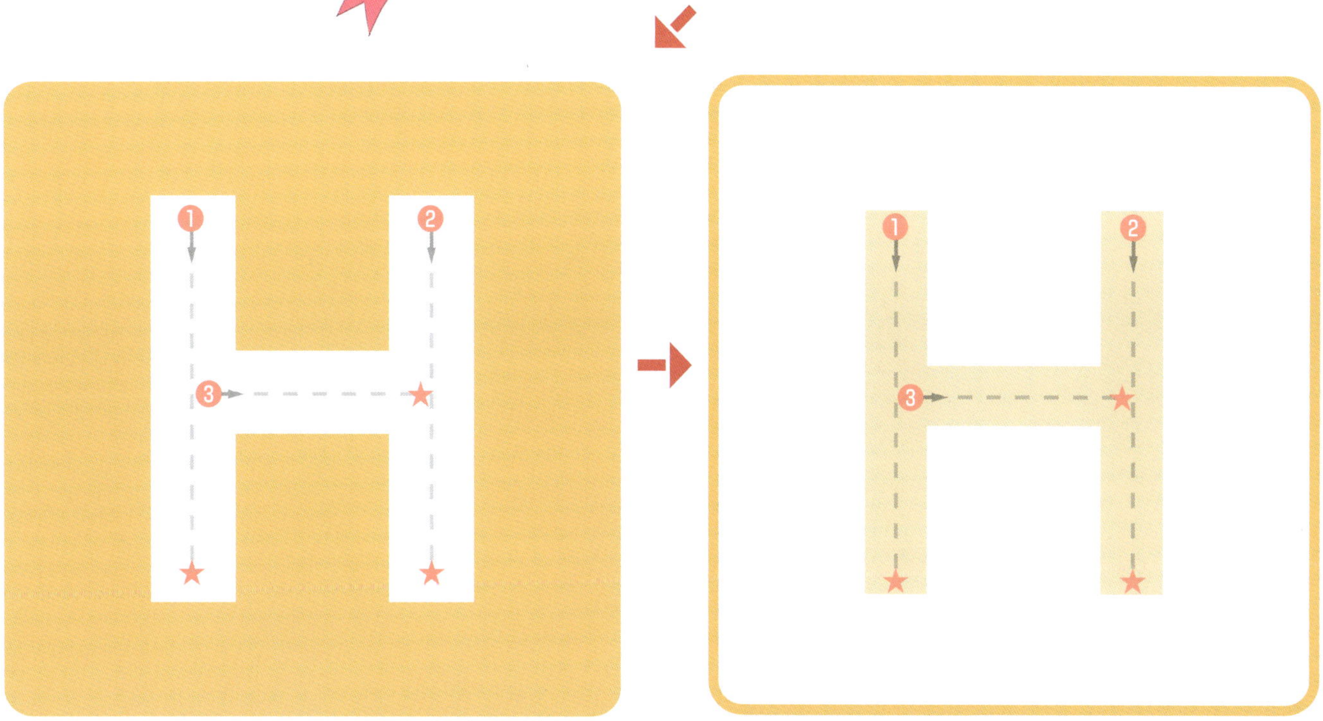

A B C D E F G **H** I J K L M N O P Q R S T U V W X Y Z

Writing L , T , and H

■ Draw a line from the dot (●) to the star (★).
Follow the order of the numbers.

LION   TOMATO   HAT

Tracing Letters
Writing I

Name

Date

■ Draw a line from the dot (●) to the star (★).
Follow the order of the numbers.

I INK

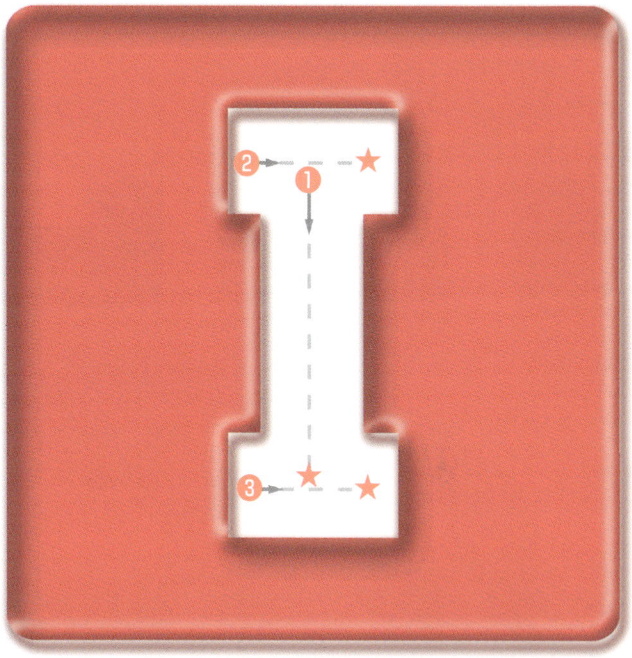

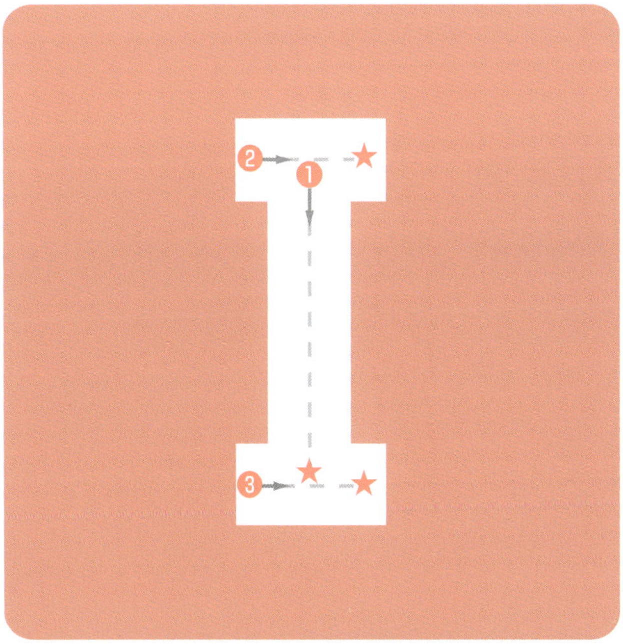

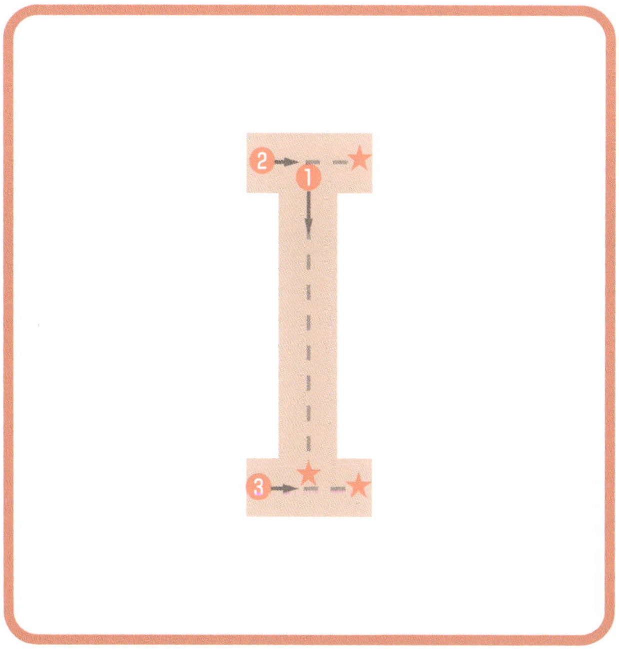

A B C D E F G H **I** J K L M N O P Q R S T U V W X Y Z

Writing F

■ Draw a line from the dot (●) to the star (★).
   Follow the order of the numbers.

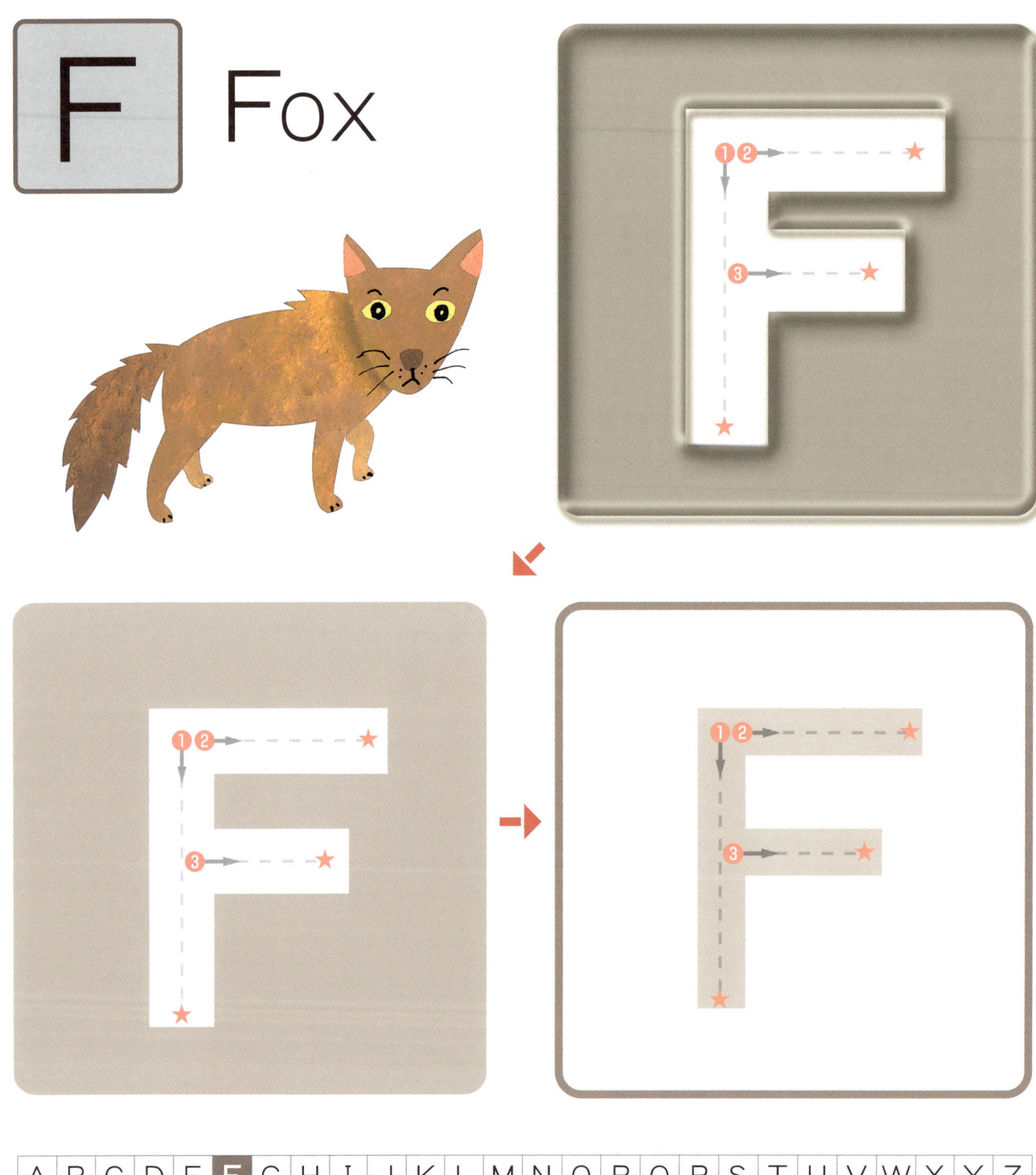

F Fox

A B C D E **F** G H I J K L M N O P Q R S T U V W X Y Z

7 Tracing Letters

Writing E

Name

Date

- Draw a line from the dot (●) to the star (★).
  Follow the order of the numbers.

E

EGG

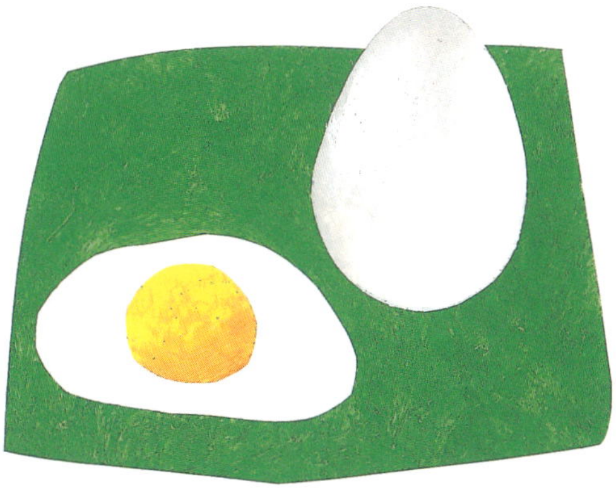

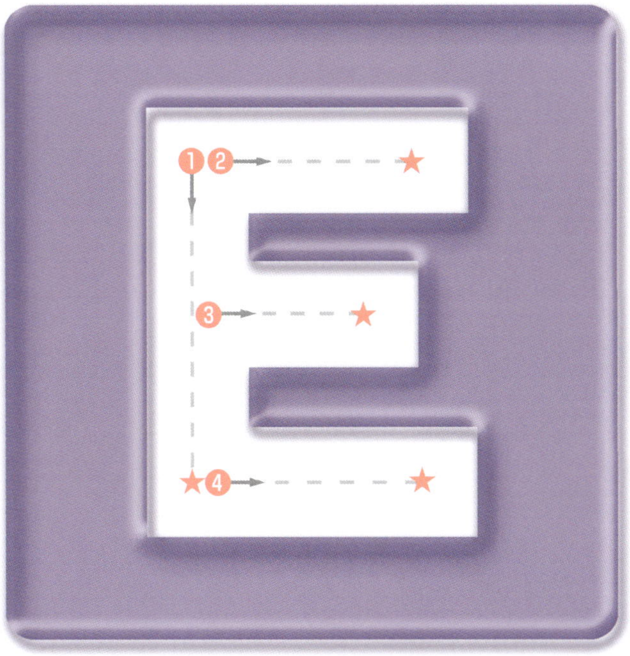

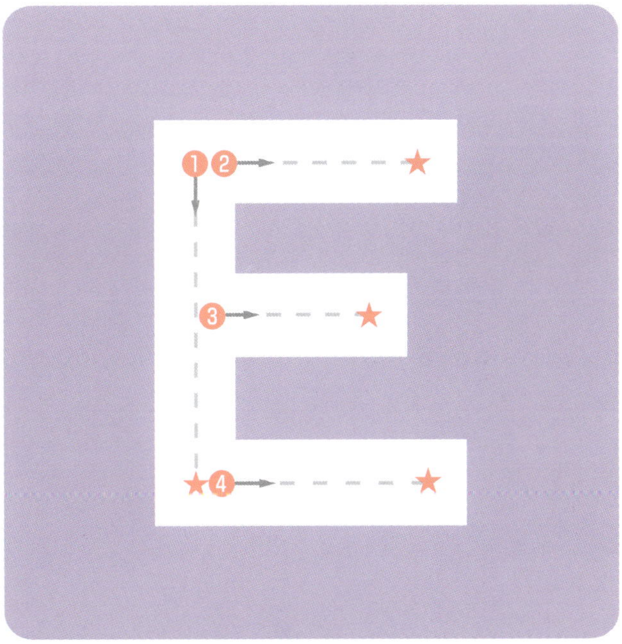

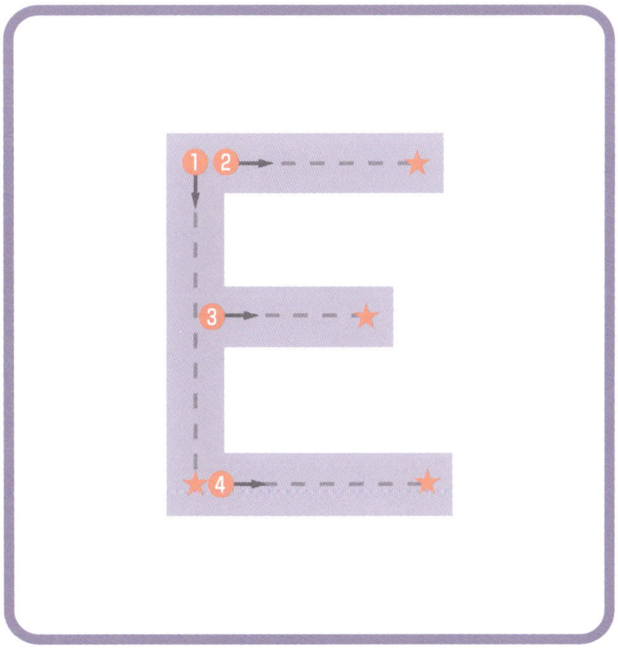

A	B	C	D	**E**	F	G	H	I	J	K	L	M	N	O	P	Q	R	S	T	U	V	W	X	Y	Z

Writing I, F, and E

■ Draw a line from the dot (●) to the star (★).
  Follow the order of the numbers.

INK   FOX   EGG

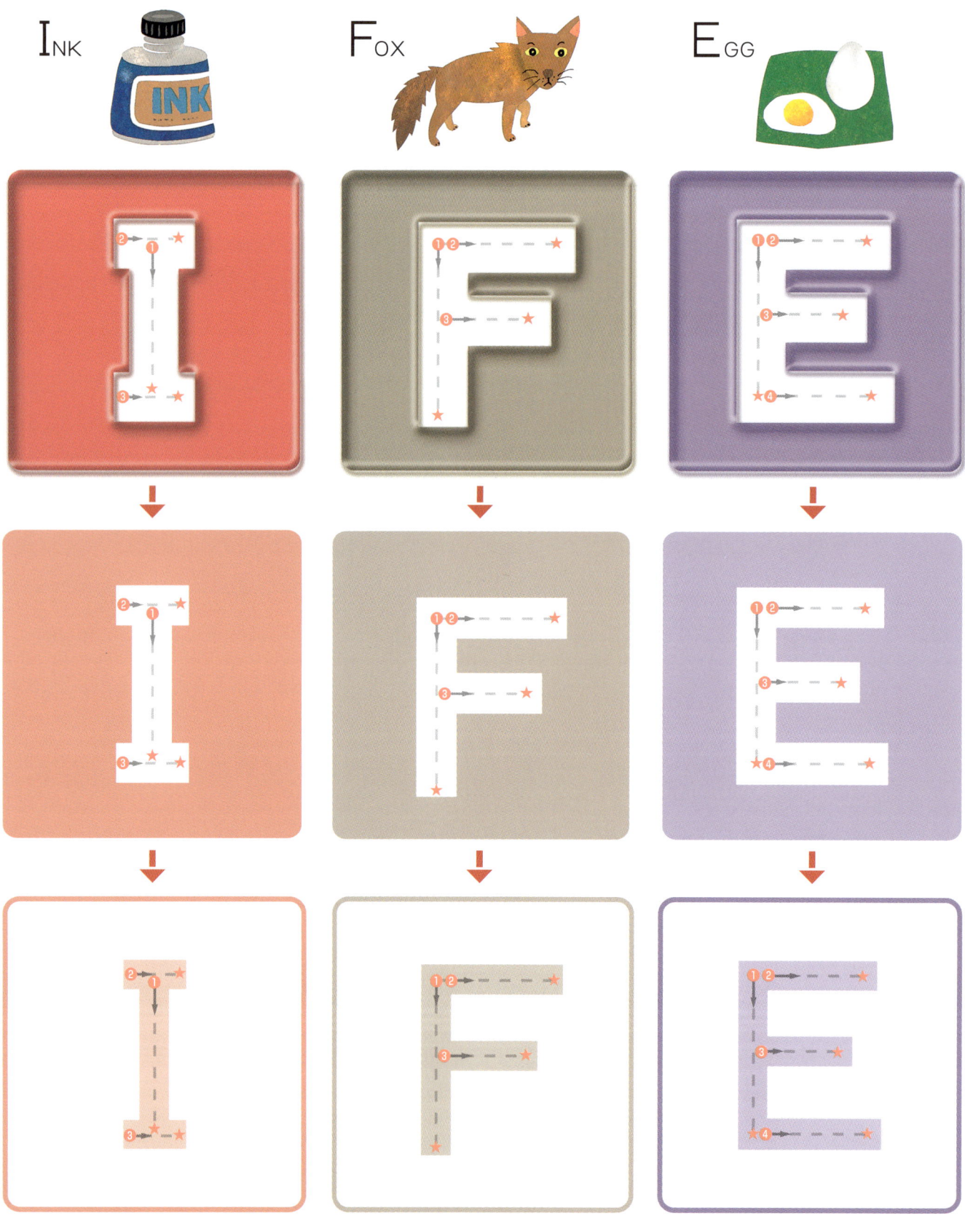

8 Review
Writing L , T , and H

■ Draw a line from the dot (●) to the star (★).
  Follow the order of the numbers.

Writing I, F, and E

■ Draw a line from the dot (●) to the star (★).
Follow the order of the numbers.

9 Drawing Right Diagonal Lines

Name

Date

■ Draw a line connecting each pair of pictures.

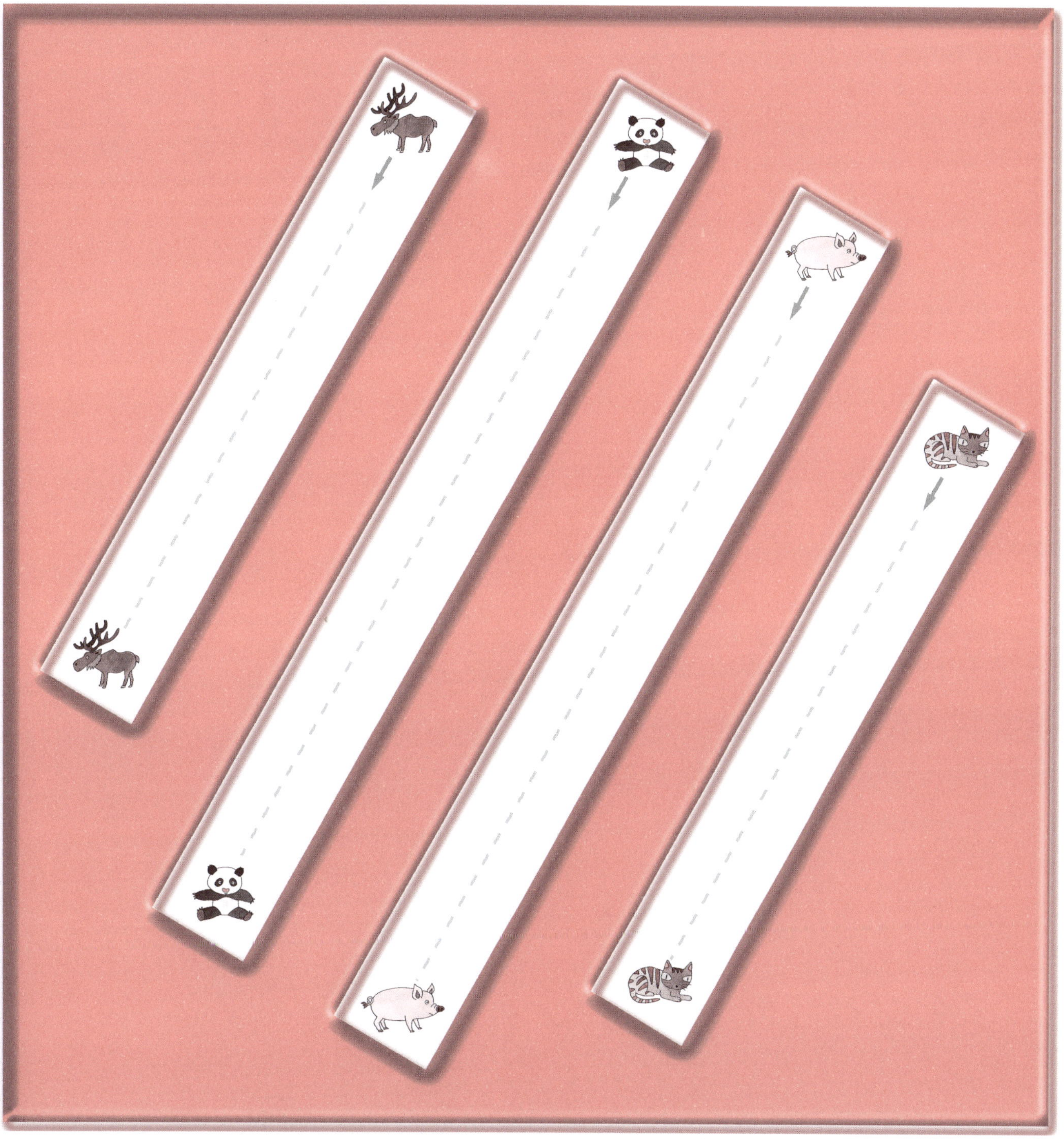

■ Draw a line connecting each pair of pictures.

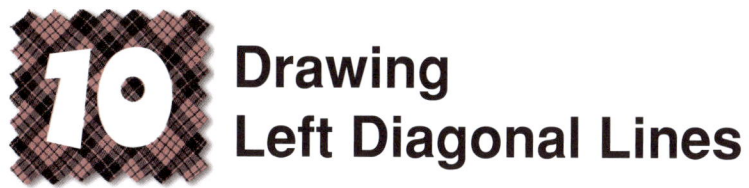

10 Drawing Left Diagonal Lines

Name

Date

■ Draw a line connecting each pair of pictures.

■ Draw a line connecting each pair of pictures.

Drawing Lines
Right Diagonal Line

Name

Date

■ Draw a line connecting each pair of pictures.

Left Diagonal Line

■ Draw a line connecting each pair of pictures.

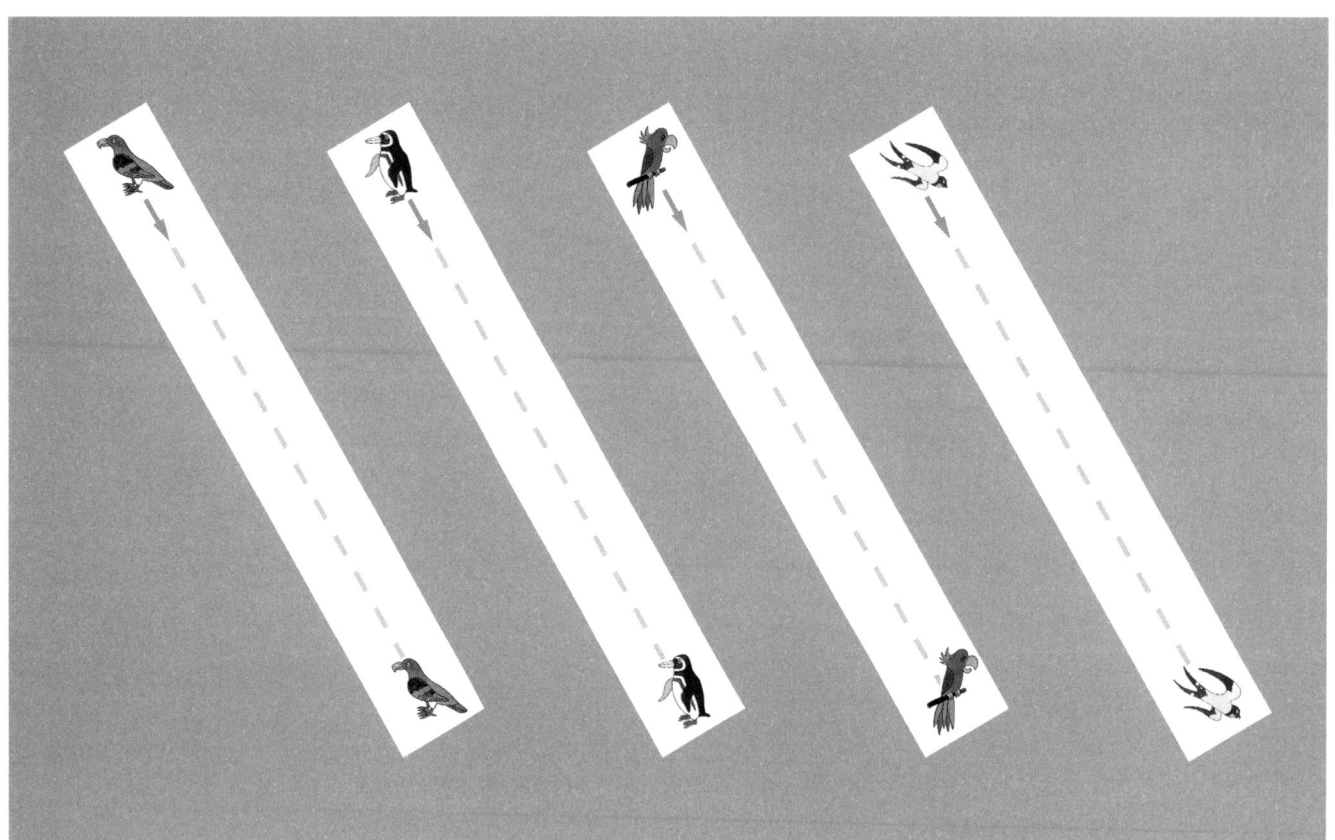

12 Tracing Letters

Writing X

Name

Date

■ Draw a line from the dot (●) to the star (★).
Follow the order of the numbers.

X

BOX

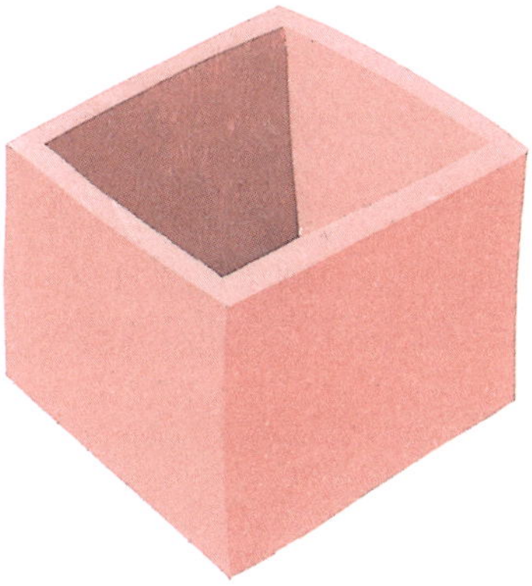

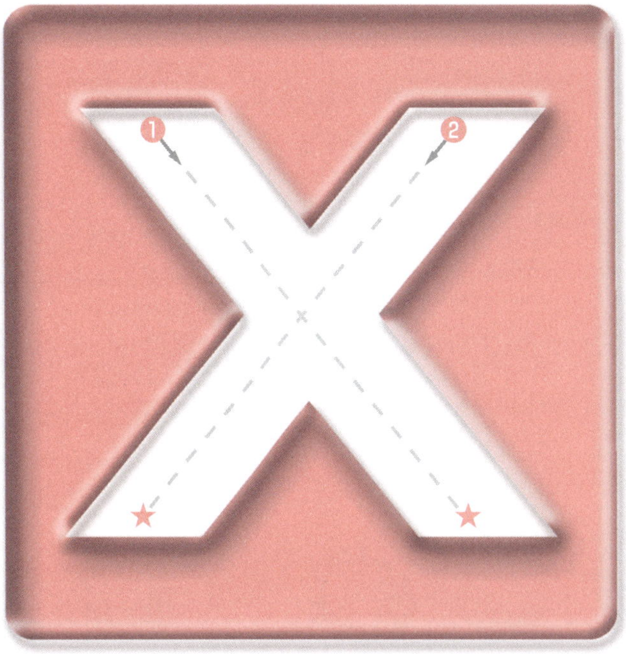

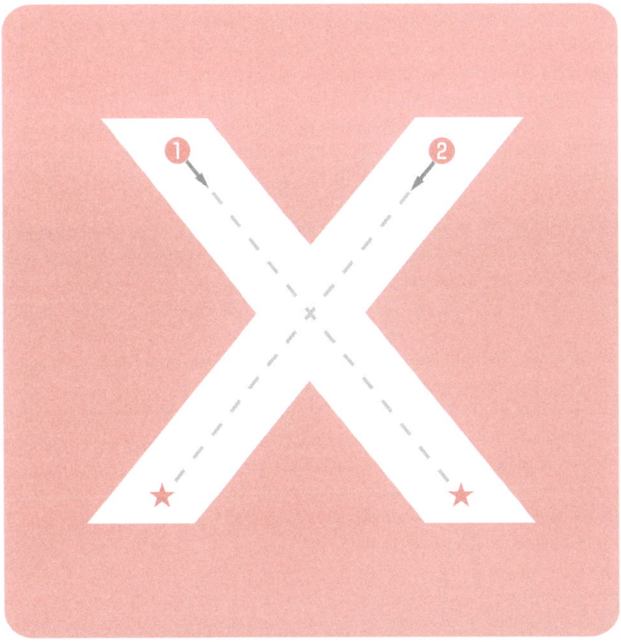

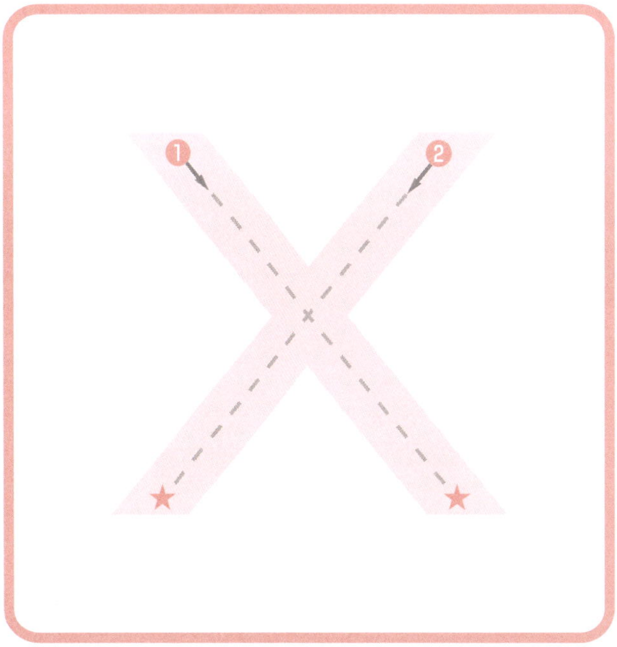

A	B	C	D	E	F	G	H	I	J	K	L	M	N	O	P	Q	R	S	T	U	V	W	X	Y	Z

Writing V

■ Draw a line from the dot (●) to the star (★).

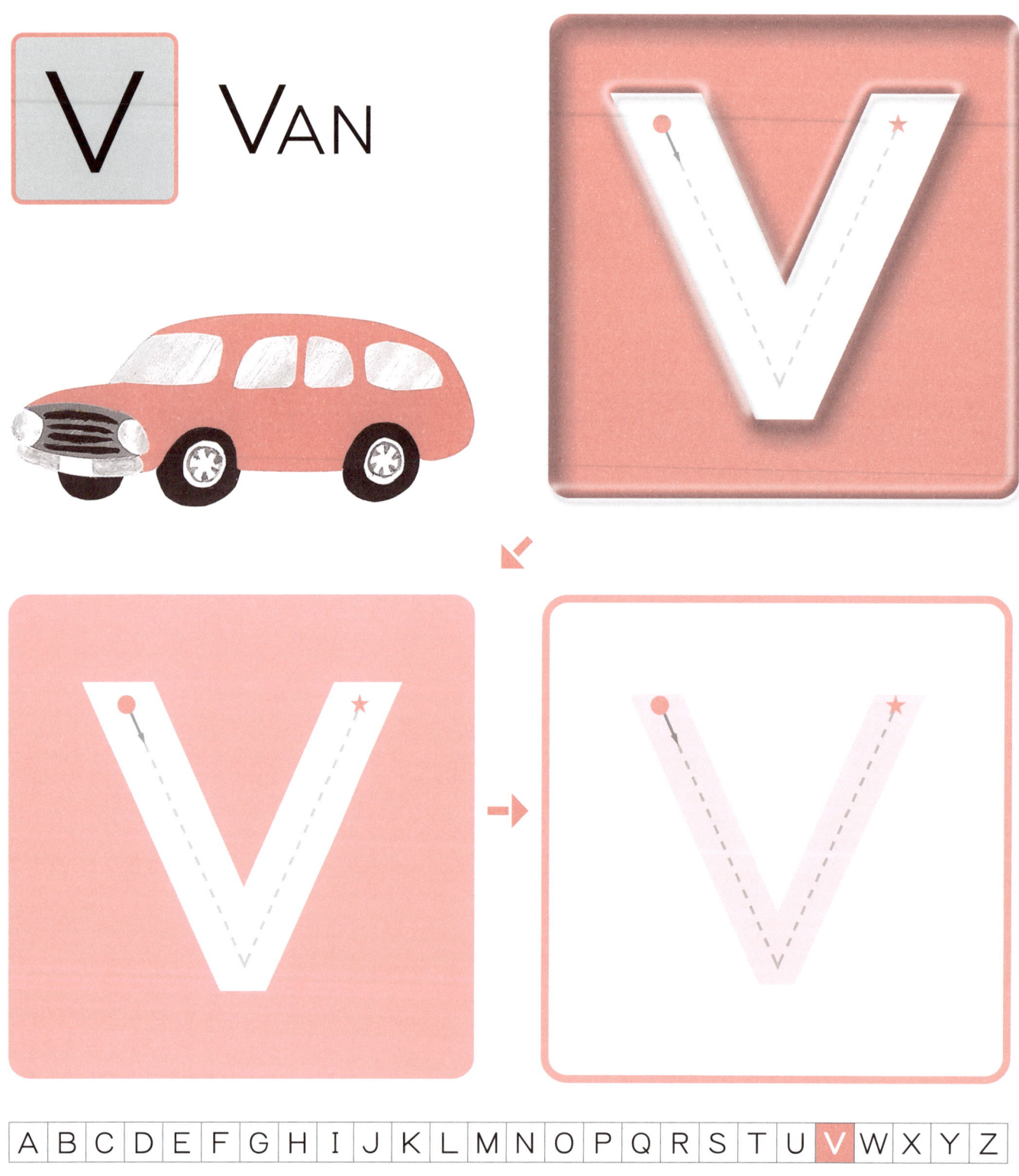

V VAN

A B C D E F G H I J K L M N O P Q R S T U **V** W X Y Z

13 Tracing Letters
Writing Y

Name

Date

- Draw a line from the dot (●) to the star (★).
Follow the order of the numbers.

Y

YACHT

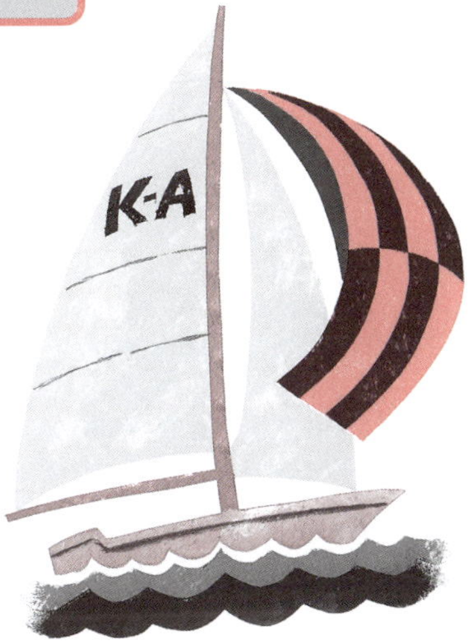

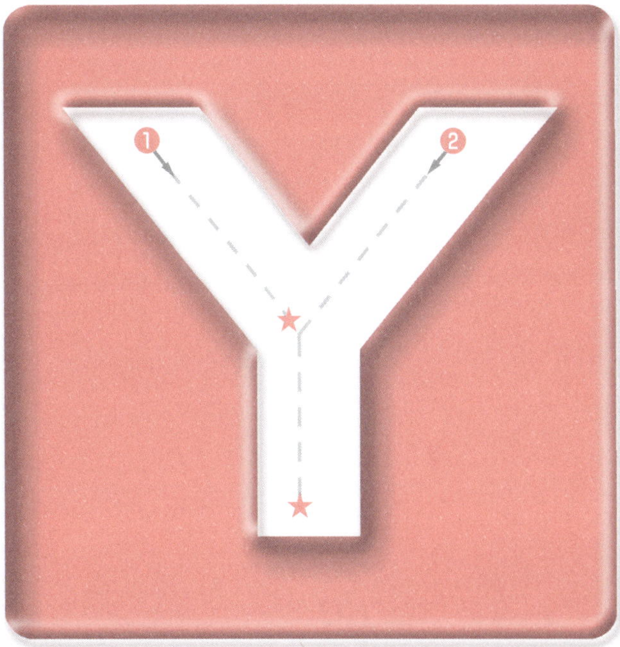

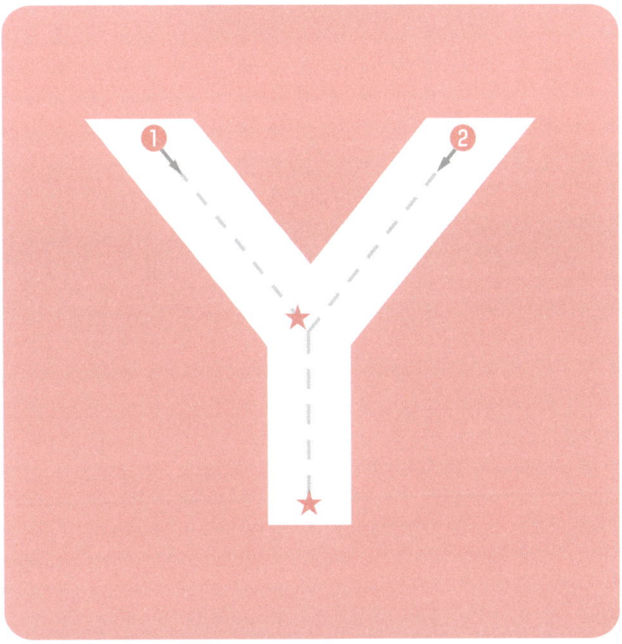

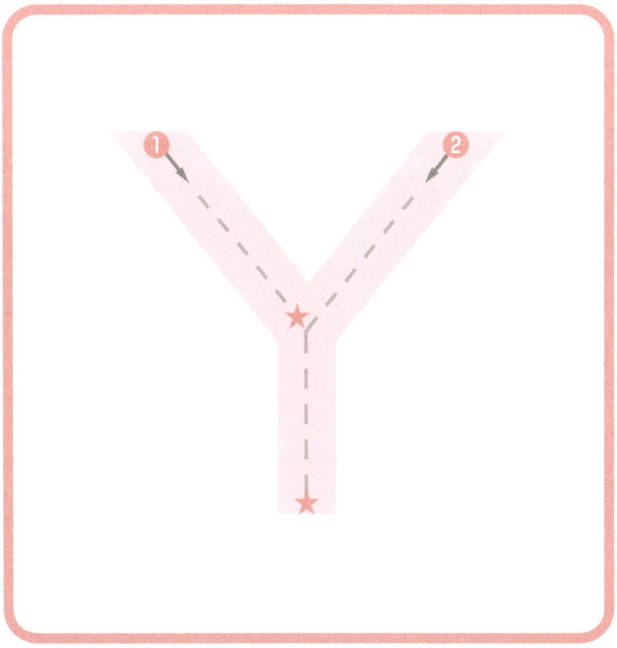

A B C D E F G H I J K L M N O P Q R S T U V W X **Y** Z

Writing X, V, and Y

■ Draw a line from the dot (●) to the star (★).
Follow the order of the numbers.

BOX   VAN   YACHT

Tracing Letters
Writing N

Name
Date

- Draw a line from the dot (●) to the star (★).
  Follow the order of the numbers.

 NUT

 →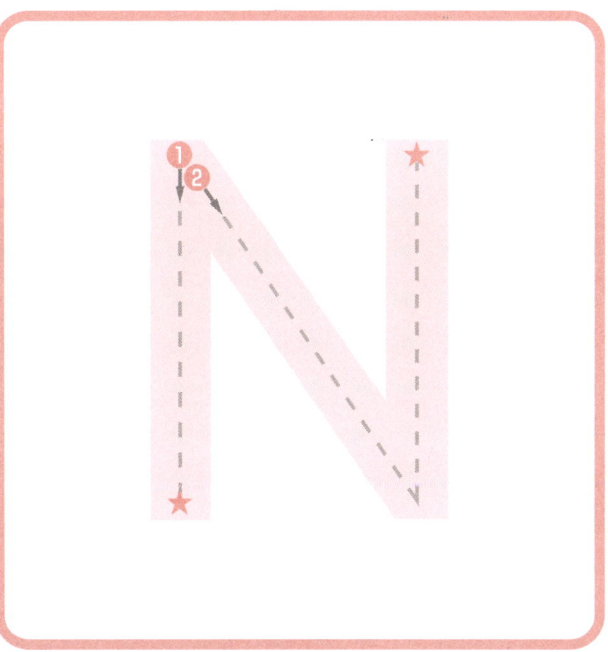

A	B	C	D	E	F	G	H	I	J	K	L	M	**N**	O	P	Q	R	S	T	U	V	W	X	Y	Z

Writing Z

- Draw a line from the dot (●) to the star (★).

A B C D E F G H I J K L M N O P Q R S T U V W X Y Z

Name
Date

■ Draw a line from the dot (●) to the star (★).
Follow the order of the numbers.

A   ANT

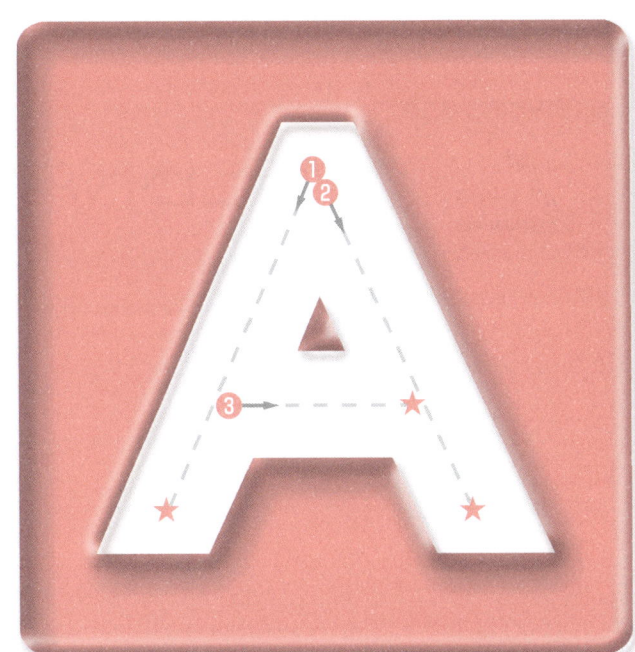

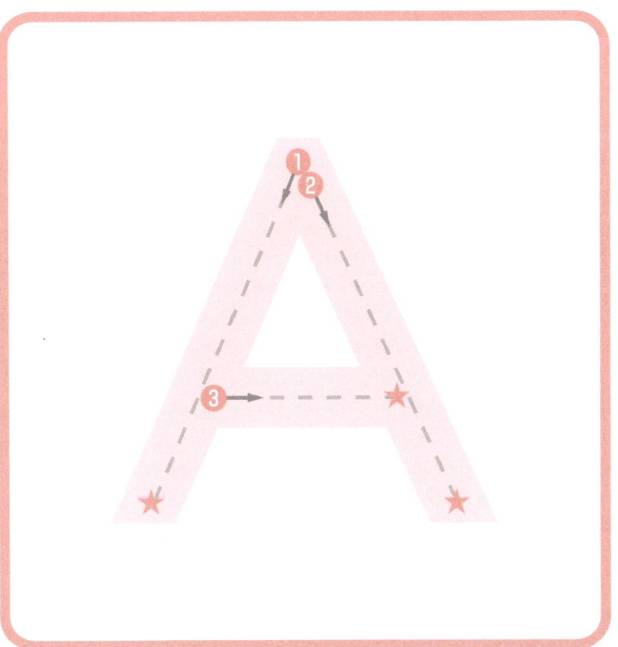

A B C D E F G H I J K L M N O P Q R S T U V W X Y Z

Writing N, Z, and A

■ Draw a line from the dot (●) to the star (★).
Follow the order of the numbers.

N_{UT} Z_{EBRA} A_{NT}

Tracing Letters
Writing K

Name

Date

■ Draw a line from the dot (●) to the star (★).
Follow the order of the numbers.

K KEY

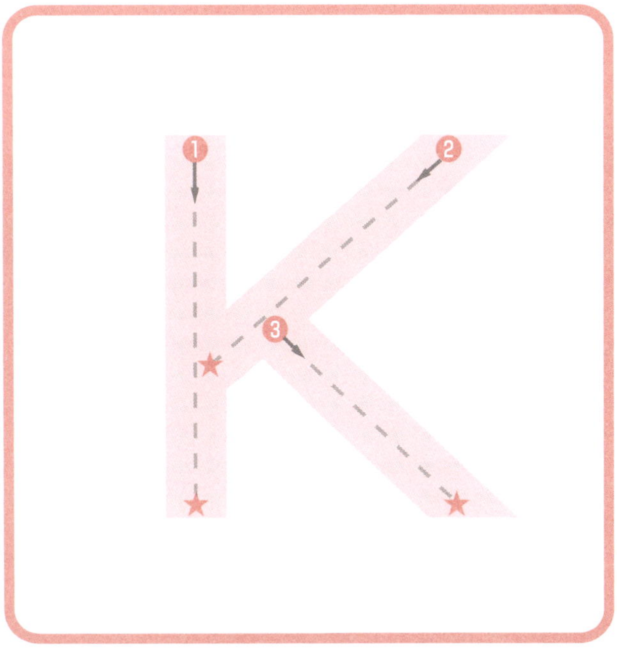

A B C D E F G H I J **K** L M N O P Q R S T U V W X Y Z

Writing M

■ Draw a line from the dot (●) to the star (★).
  Follow the order of the numbers.

M MAT

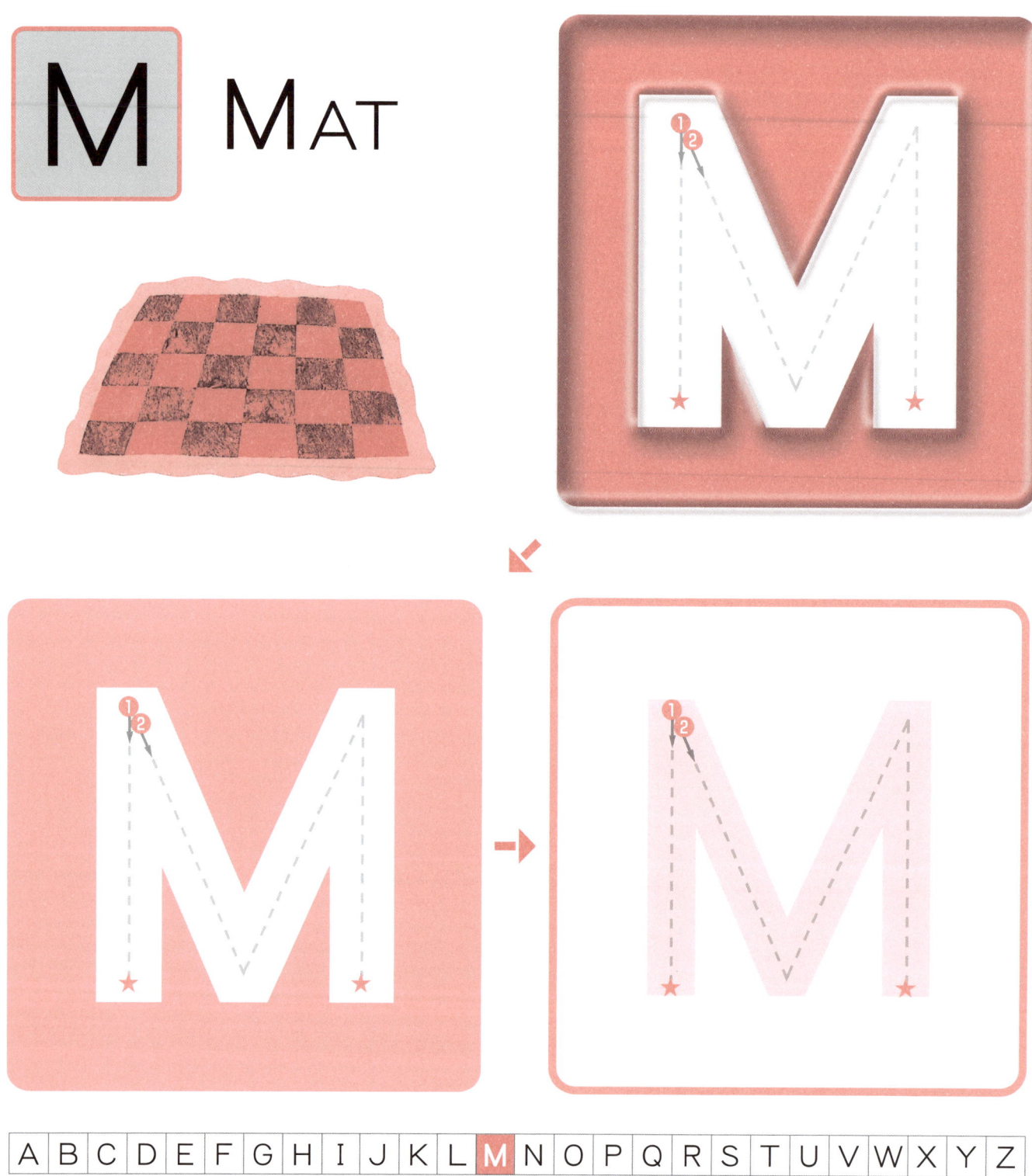

| A | B | C | D | E | F | G | H | I | J | K | L | M | N | O | P | Q | R | S | T | U | V | W | X | Y | Z |

17 Tracing Letters
Writing W

Name

Date

■ Draw a line from the dot (●) to the star (★).

W WATER

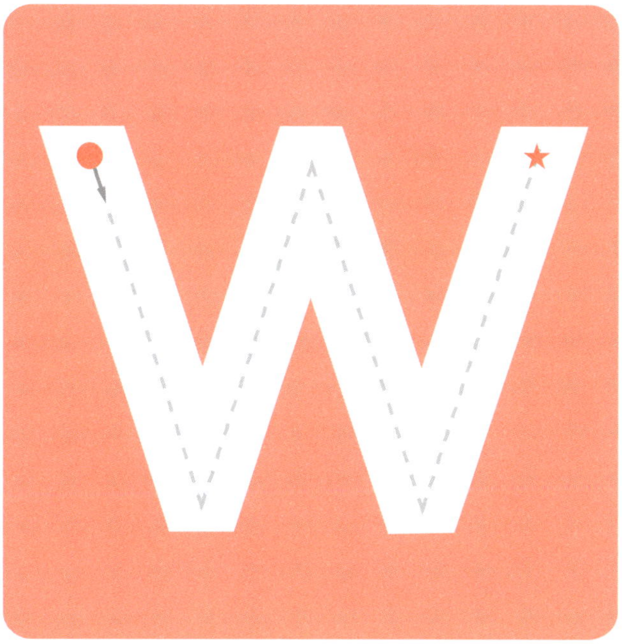

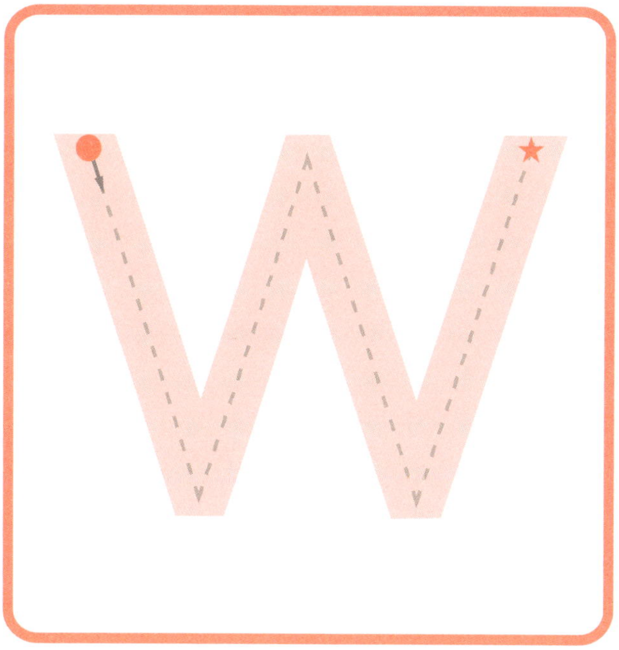

A	B	C	D	E	F	G	H	I	J	K	L	M	N	O	P	Q	R	S	T	U	V	W	X	Y	Z

Writing K, M, and W

- Draw a line from the dot (●) to the star (★).
  Follow the order of the numbers.

K_{EY}   M_{AT}   W_{ATER}

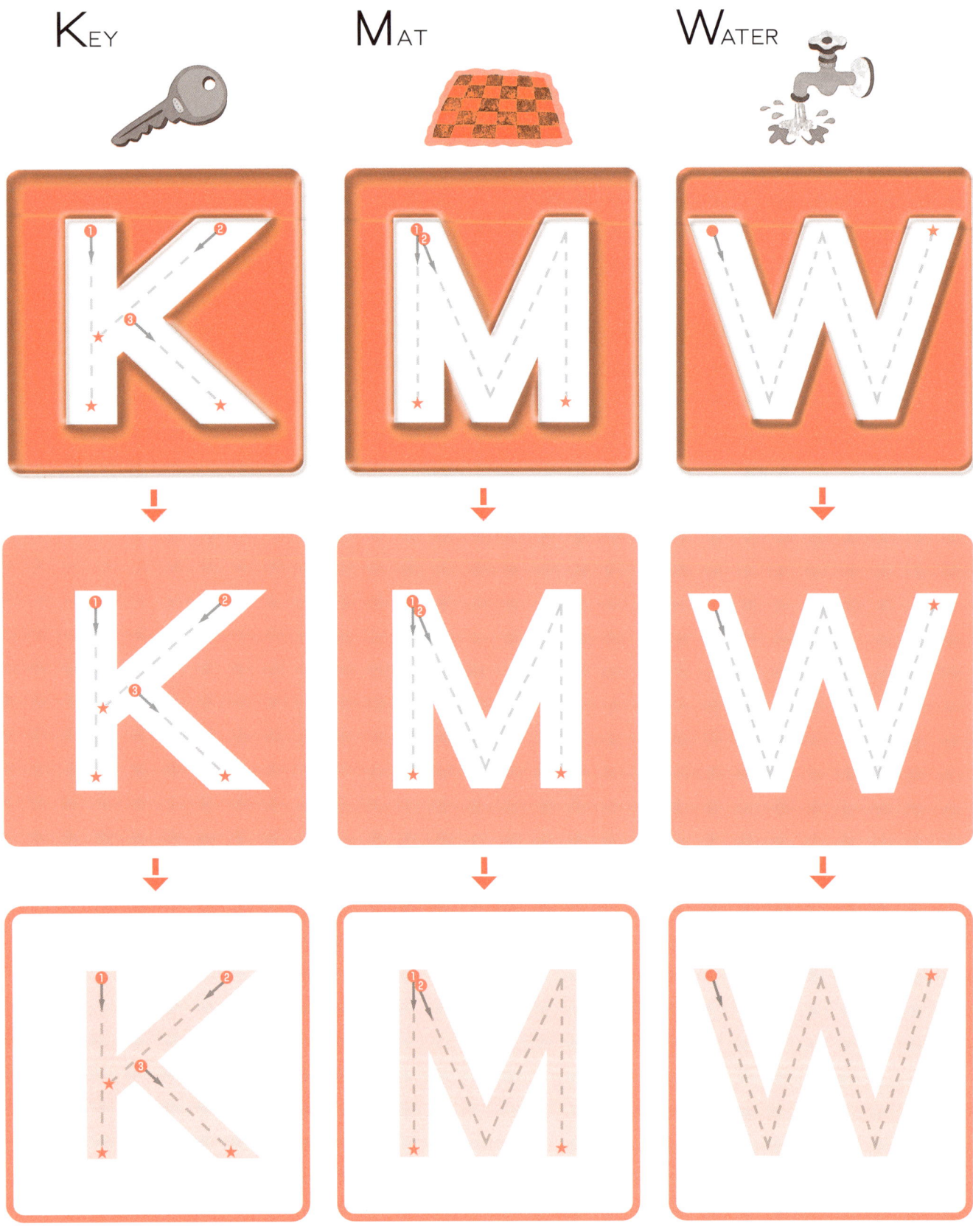

18 Review
Writing X, V, and Y

Name

Date

■ Draw a line from the dot (●) to the star (★).
Follow the order of the numbers.

Writing N, Z, and A

■ Draw a line from the dot (●) to the star (★).
Follow the order of the numbers.

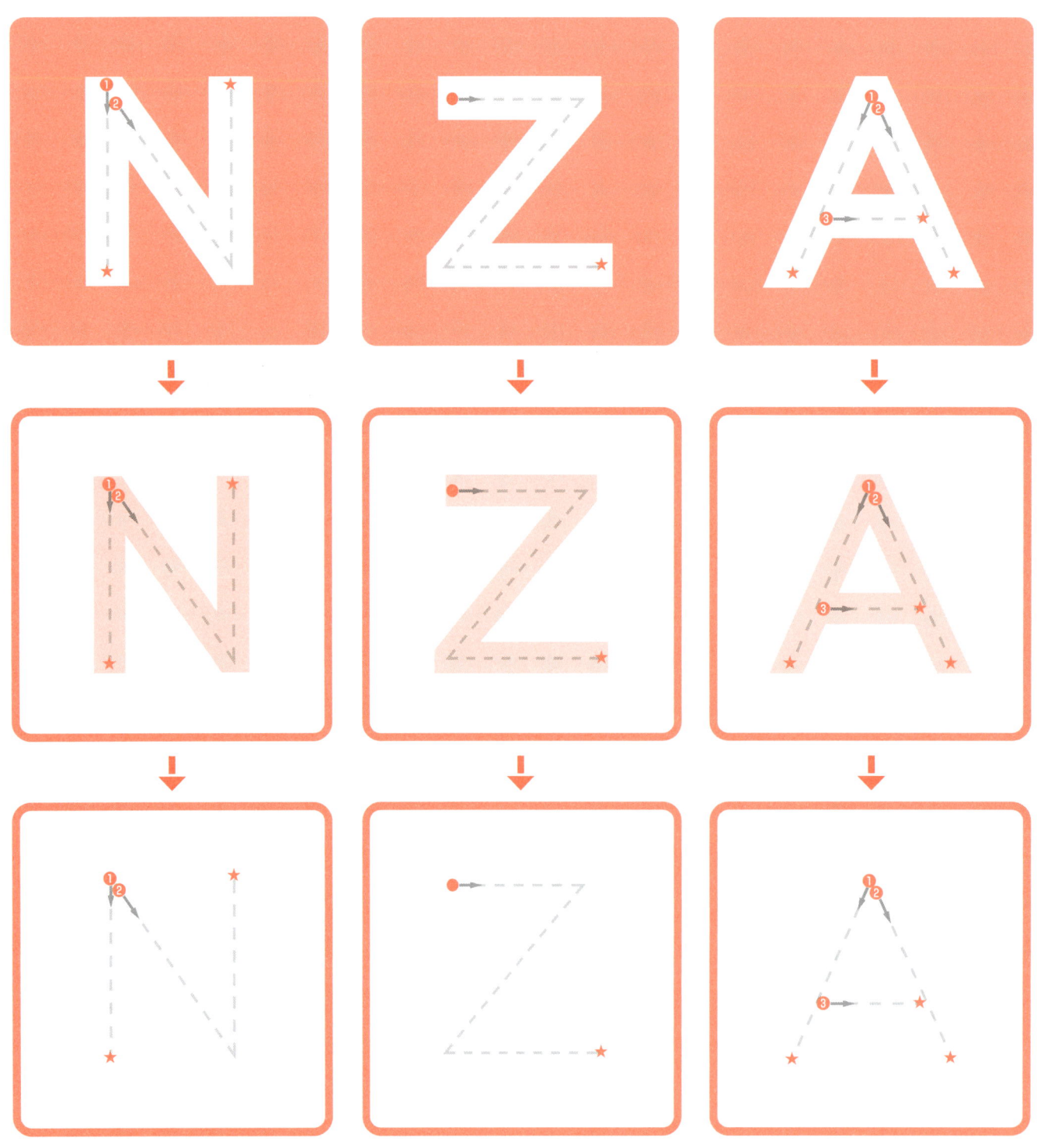

Review

Writing K, M, and W

■ Draw a line from the dot (●) to the star (★).
  Follow the order of the numbers.

■ Trace the letters below.

20 Drawing Right Curved Lines

Name

Date

■ Draw a line connecting each pair of pictures.

Draw a line connecting each pair of pictures.

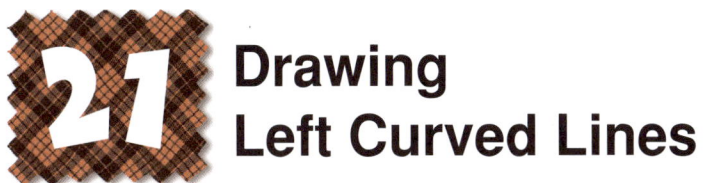

21 Drawing Left Curved Lines

Name

Date

■ Draw a line connecting each pair of pictures.

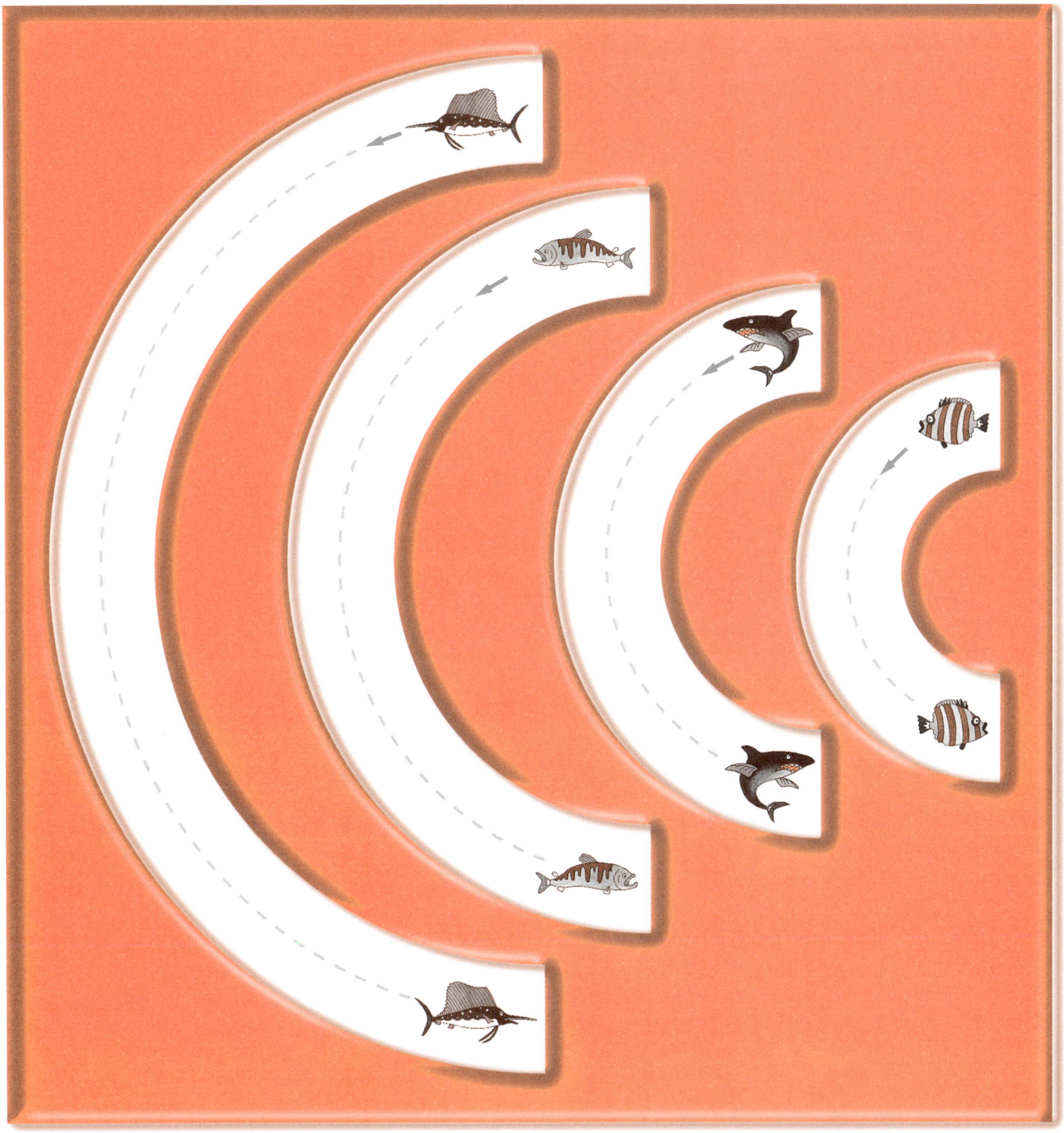

Draw a line connecting each pair of pictures.

22 Drawing Lines
Right Curved Line

Name

Date

■ Draw a line connecting each pair of pictures.

Left Curved Line

■ Draw a line connecting each pair of pictures.

Tracing Letters
Writing D

Name

Date

■ Draw a line from the dot (●) to the star (★).
Follow the order of the numbers.

D **D**OG

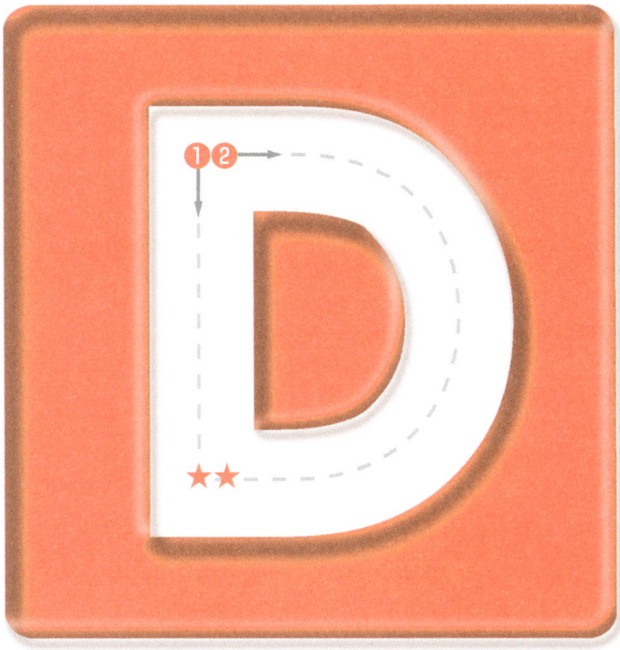

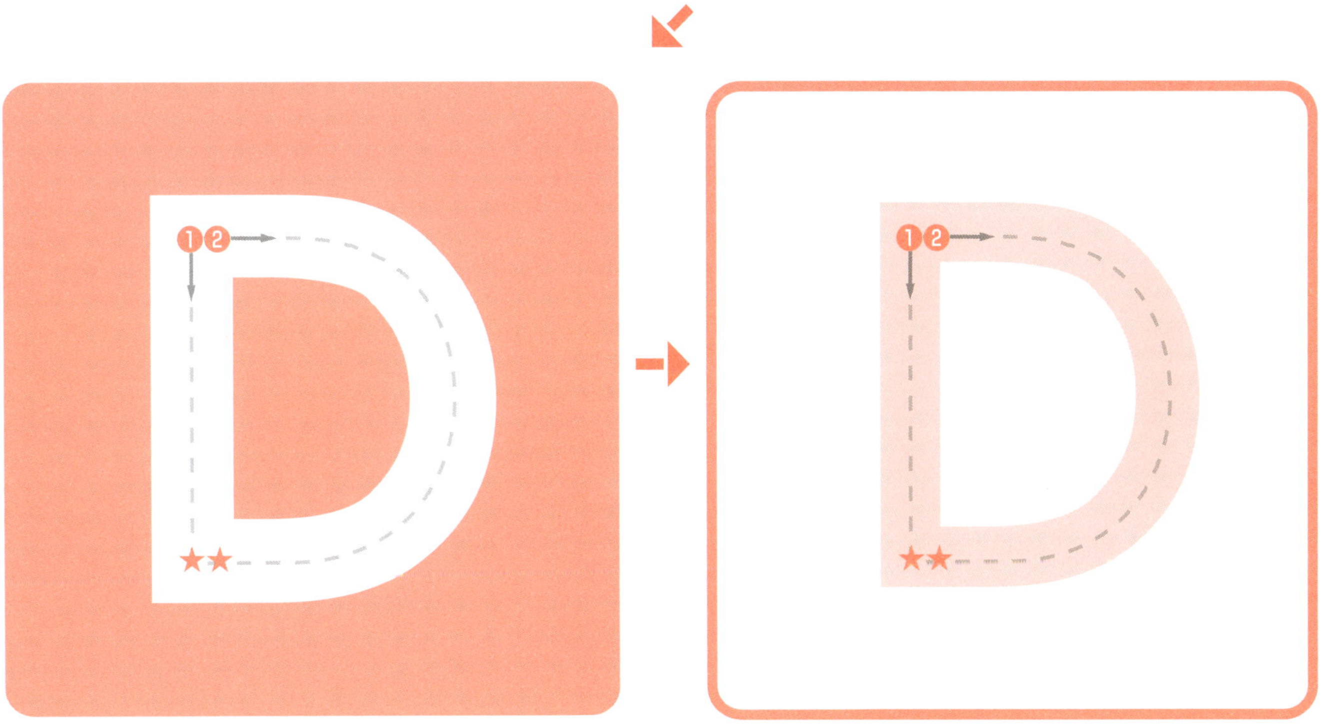

| A | B | C | D | E | F | G | H | I | J | K | L | M | N | O | P | Q | R | S | T | U | V | W | X | Y | Z |

Writing D

45

Writing P

■ Draw a line from the dot (●) to the star (★).
Follow the order of the numbers.

P P PAN

| A | B | C | D | E | F | G | H | I | J | K | L | M | N | O | **P** | Q | R | S | T | U | V | W | X | Y | Z |

Tracing Letters
Writing B

Name

Date

■ Draw a line from the dot (●) to the star (★).
Follow the order of the numbers.

 BAG

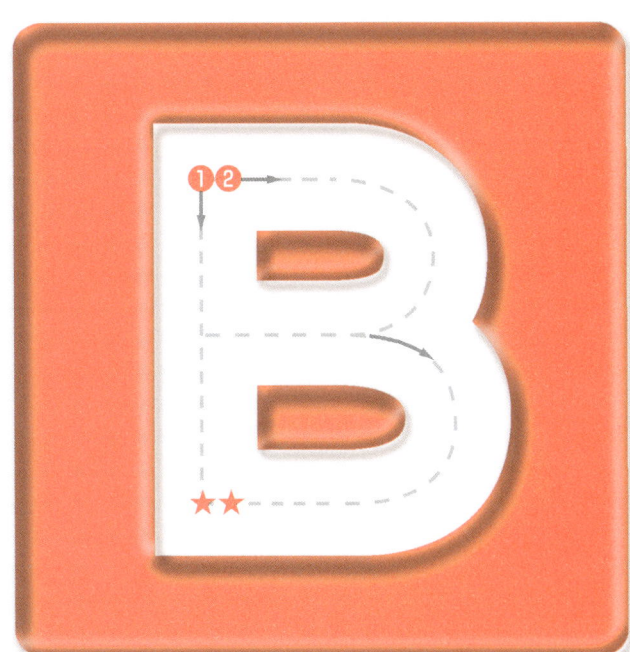

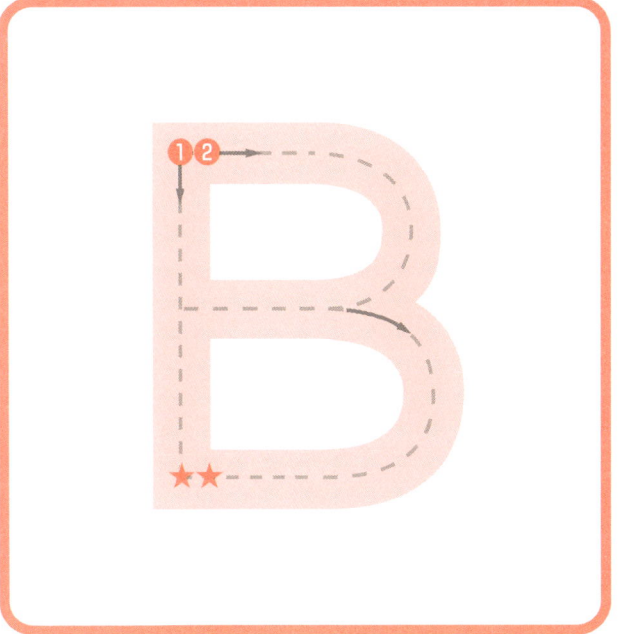

| A | B | C | D | E | F | G | H | I | J | K | L | M | N | O | P | Q | R | S | T | U | V | W | X | Y | Z |

Writing D, P, and B

■ Draw a line from the dot (●) to the star (★).
Follow the order of the numbers.

D_{OG}　　　P_{AN}　　　B_{AG}

Tracing Letters
Writing R

Name

Date

■ Draw a line from the dot (●) to the star (★).
Follow the order of the numbers.

R RAT

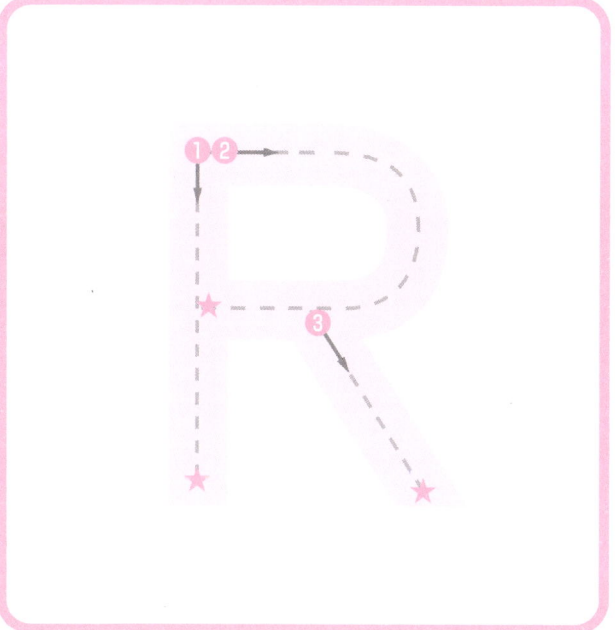

| A | B | C | D | E | F | G | H | I | J | K | L | M | N | O | P | Q | R | S | T | U | V | W | X | Y | Z |

Writing J

- Draw a line from the dot (●) to the star (★).

J JAM

A B C D E F G H I **J** K L M N O P Q R S T U V W X Y Z

Tracing Letters
Writing U

■ Draw a line from the dot (●) to the star (★).

U Up

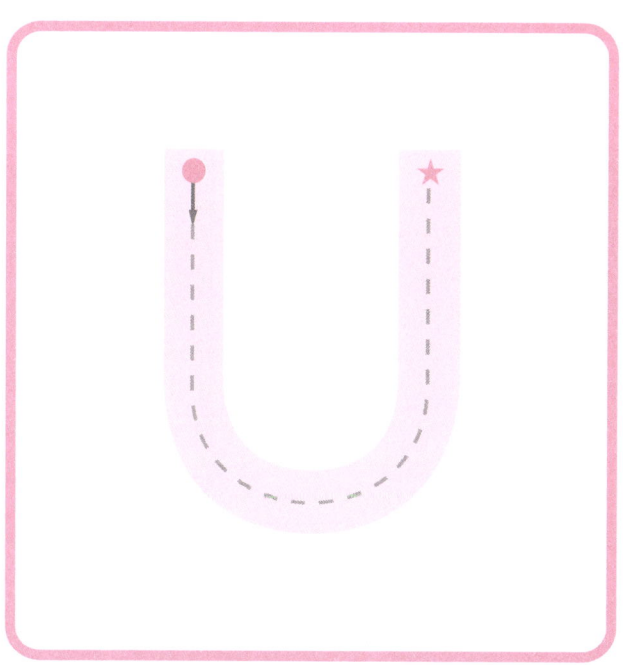

A B C D E F G H I J K L M N O P Q R S T **U** V W X Y Z

Writing R, J, and U

■ Draw a line from the dot (●) to the star (★).
Follow the order of the numbers.

R_{AT}   J_{AM}   U_P

Review

Writing D, P, and B

Name

Date

■ Draw a line from the dot (●) to the star (★).
Follow the order of the numbers.

Writing D, P, and B

53

Writing R, J, and U

■ Draw a line from the dot (●) to the star (★).
Follow the order of the numbers.

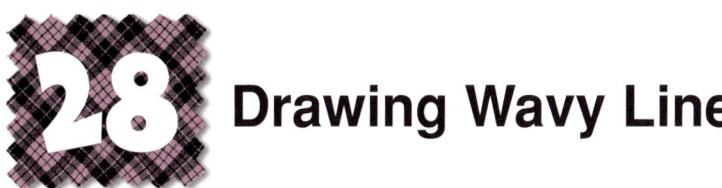

28 Drawing Wavy Lines

Name

Date

- Draw a line connecting each pair of pictures.

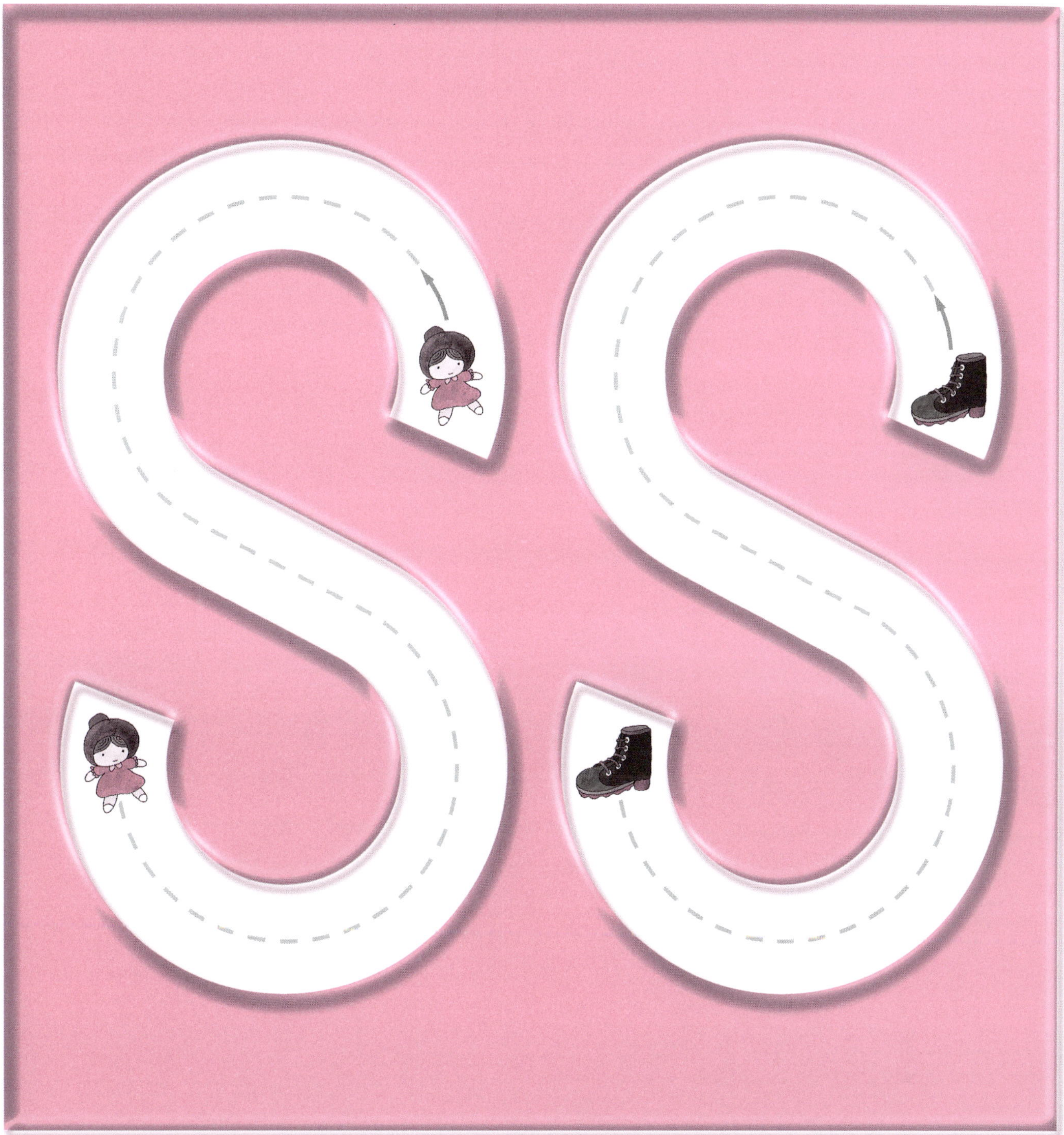

■ Draw a line connecting each pair of pictures.

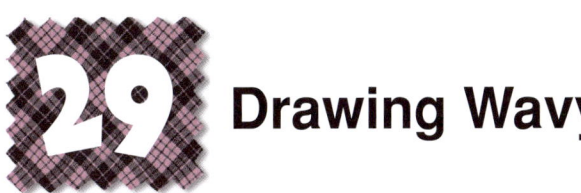

29 Drawing Wavy Lines

Name
Date

- Draw a line connecting each pair of pictures.

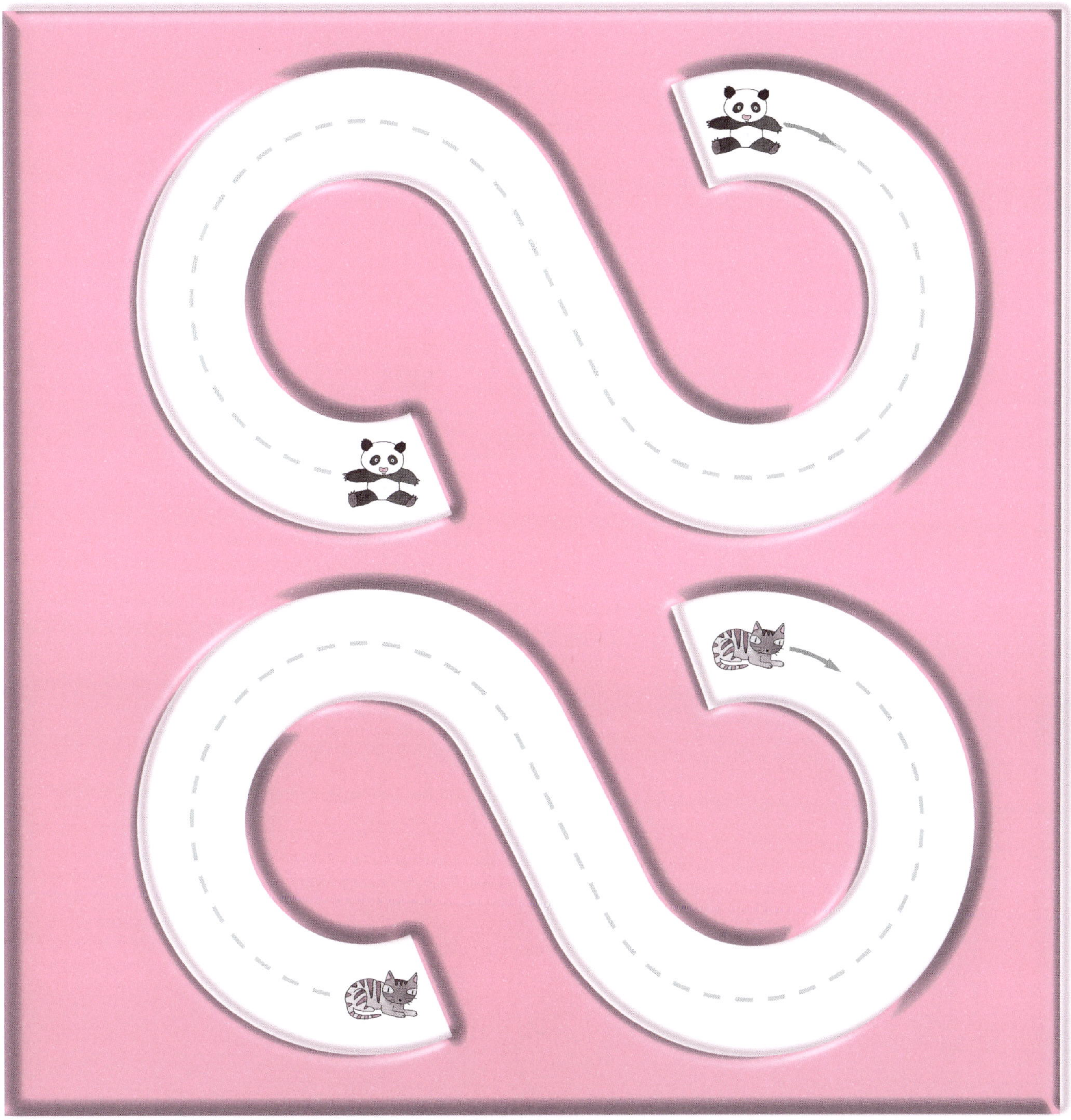

■ Draw a line connecting each pair of pictures.

30 Tracing Letters
Writing C

Name

Date

■ Draw a line from the dot (●) to the star (★).

C

CAT

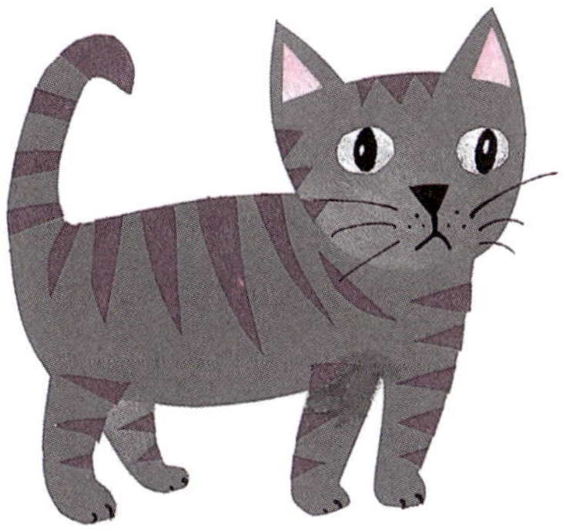

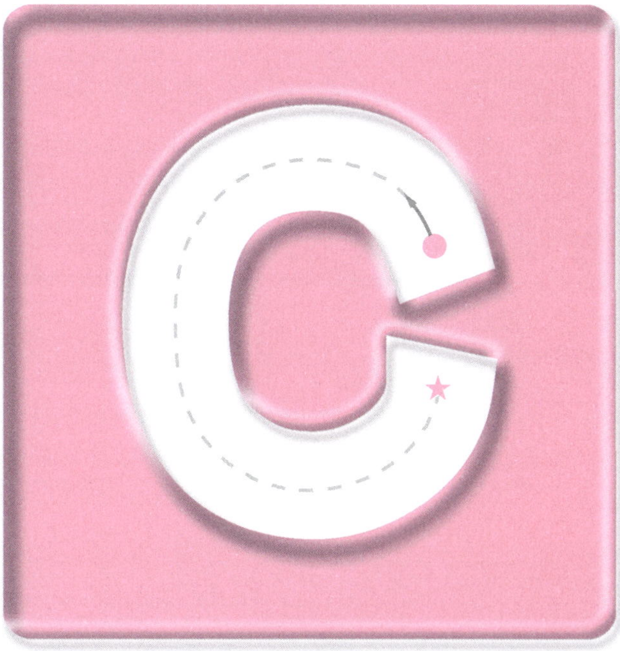

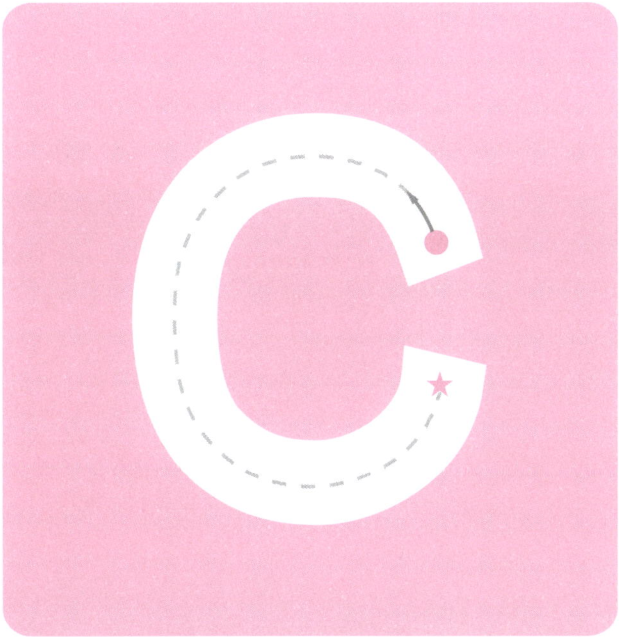

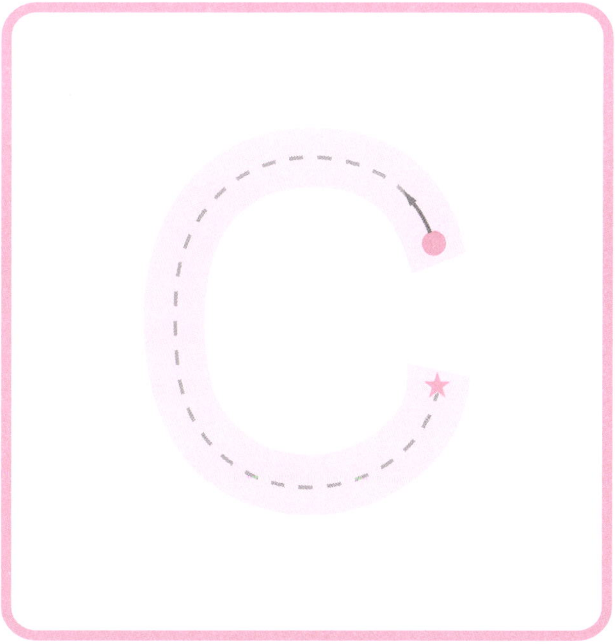

A B C D E F G H I J K L M N O P Q R S T U V W X Y Z

Writing G

■ Draw a line from the dot (●) to the star (★).
Follow the order of the numbers.

G GIFT

| A | B | C | D | E | F | G | H | I | J | K | L | M | N | O | P | Q | R | S | T | U | V | W | X | Y | Z |

31 Tracing Letters
Writing S

Name

Date

■ Draw a line from the dot (●) to the star (★).

S

SUN

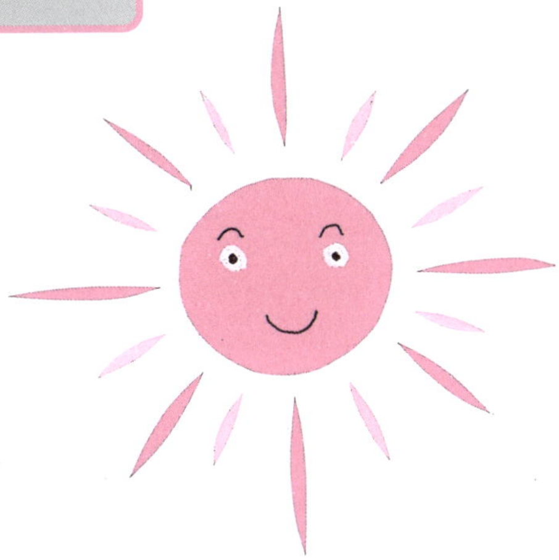

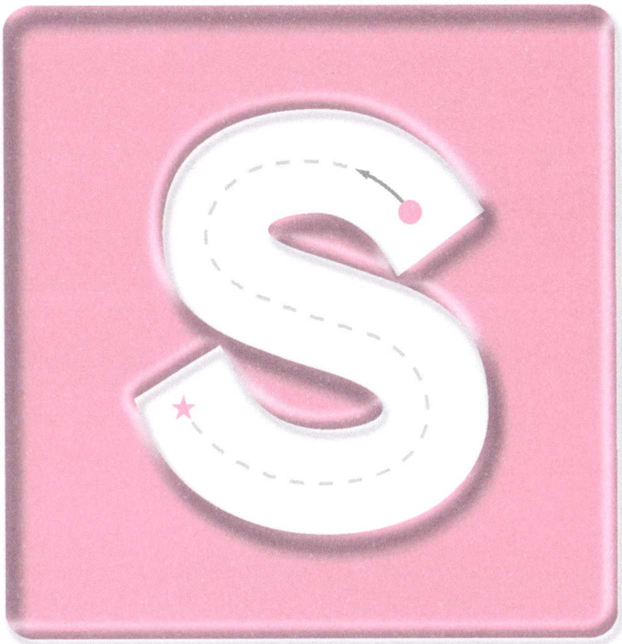

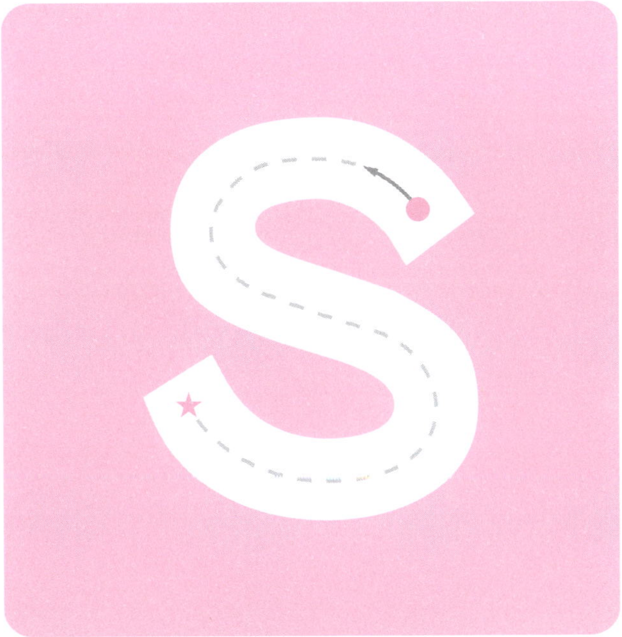

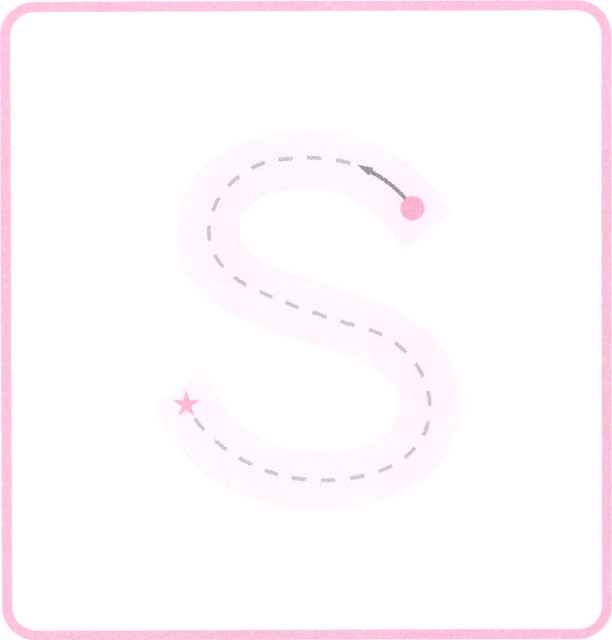

A	B	C	D	E	F	G	H	I	J	K	L	M	N	O	P	Q	R	S	T	U	V	W	X	Y	Z

Writing C, G, and S

- Draw a line from the dot (●) to the star (★).
  Follow the order of the numbers.

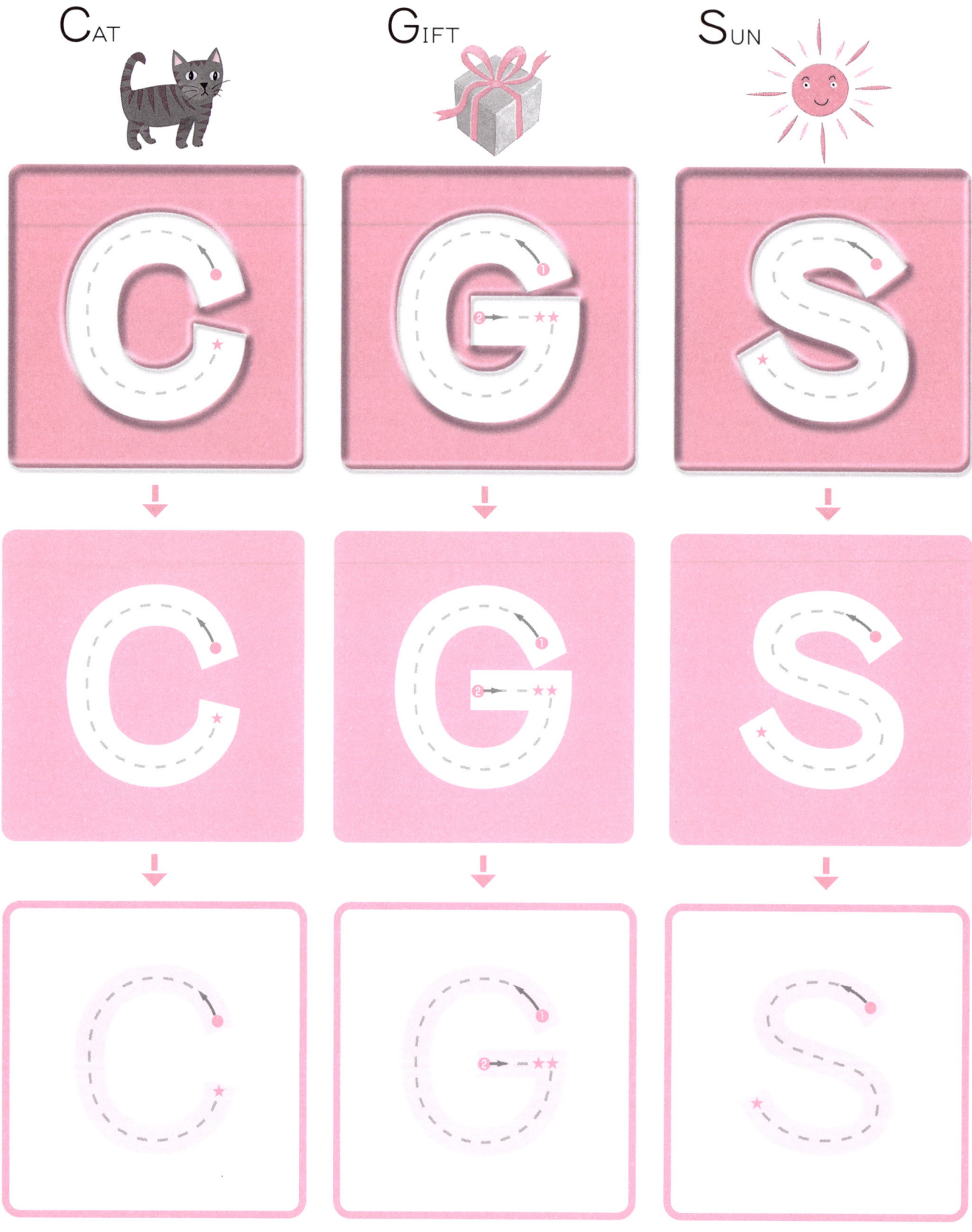

C_{AT} G_{IFT} S_{UN}

32 Drawing Circle Lines

Name
Date

■ Draw a line connecting each pair of pictures.

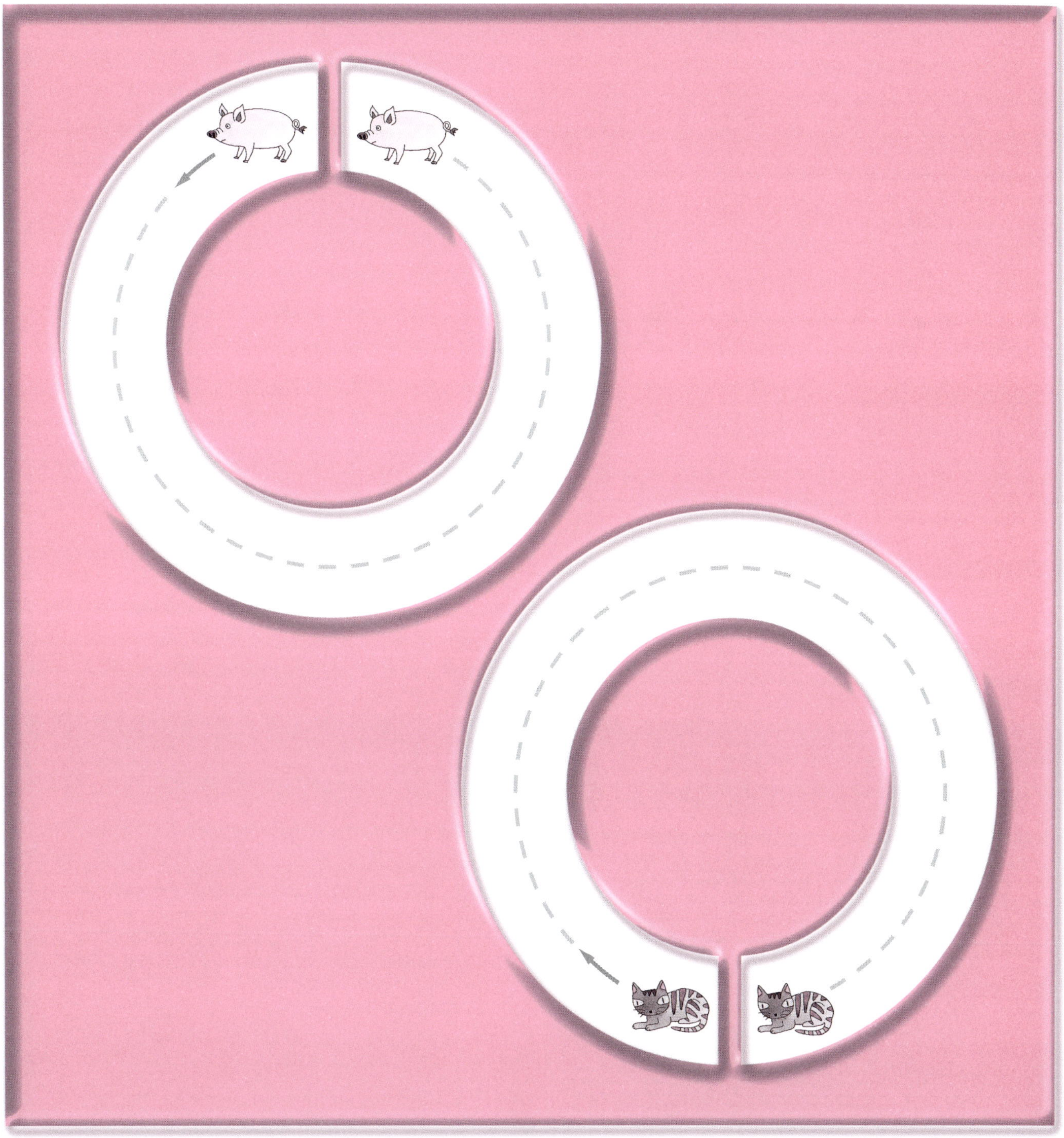

Draw a line connecting each pair of pictures.

33 Tracing Letters
Writing O

Name

Date

■ Draw a line from the dot (●) to the star (★).

O ORANGE

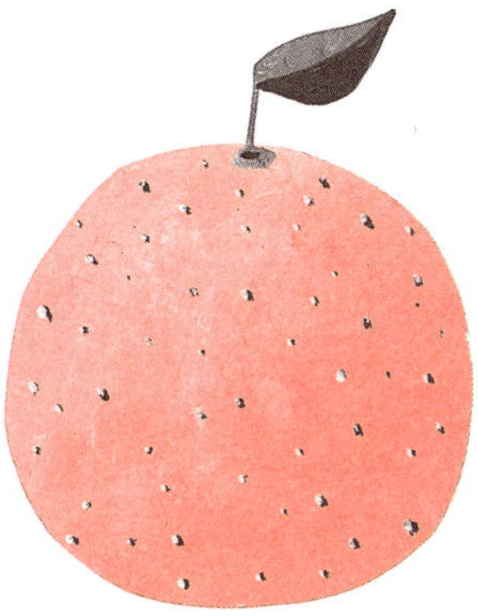

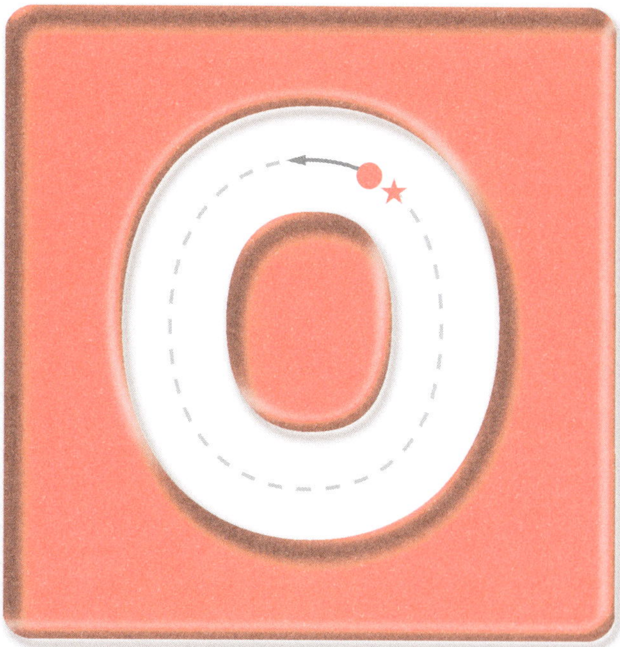

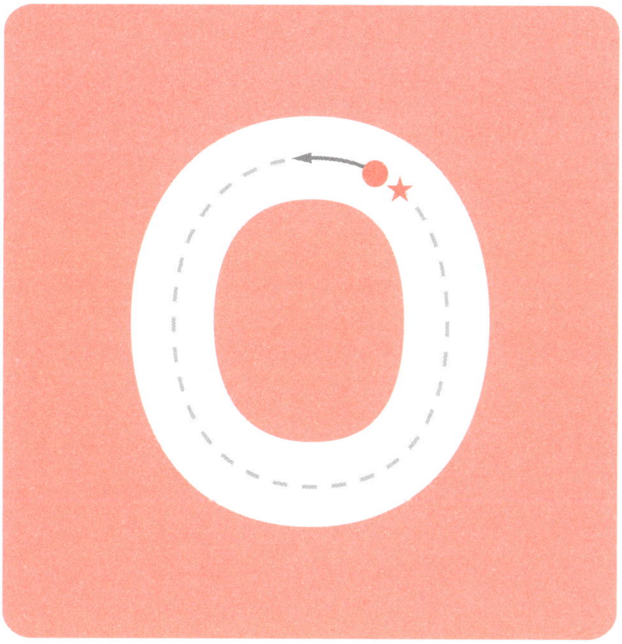

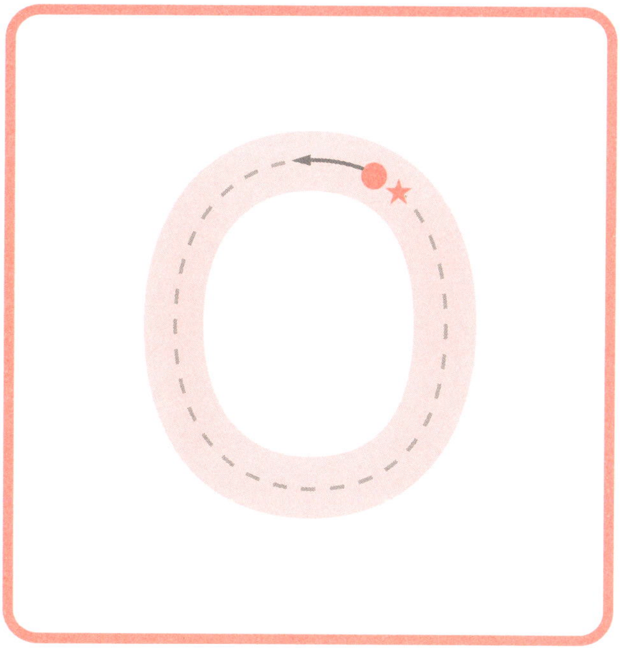

A	B	C	D	E	F	G	H	I	J	K	L	M	N	O	P	Q	R	S	T	U	V	W	X	Y	Z

Writing Q

■ Draw a line from the dot (●) to the star (★).
  Follow the order of the numbers.

Q QUEEN

A B C D E F G H I J K L M N O P Q R S T U V W X Y Z

Review
Writing C, G, and S

Name

Date

■ Draw a line from the dot (●) to the star (★).
Follow the order of the numbers.

Writing O and Q

■ Draw a line from the dot (●) to the star (★).
  Follow the order of the numbers.

35 Review

■ Trace the letters below.

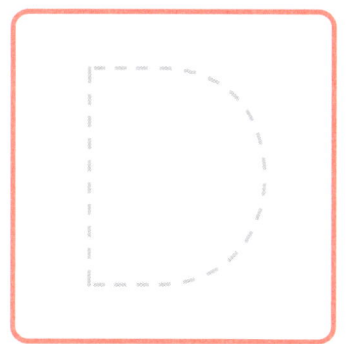
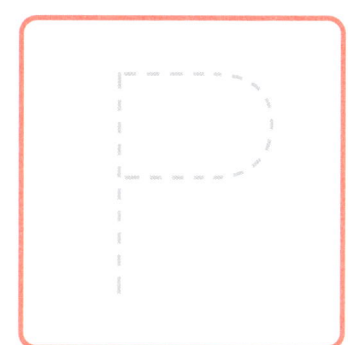

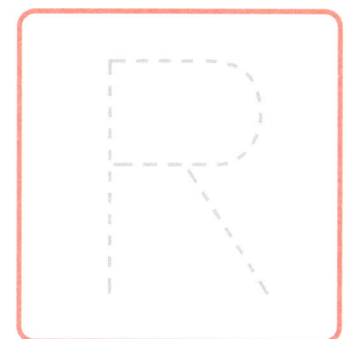
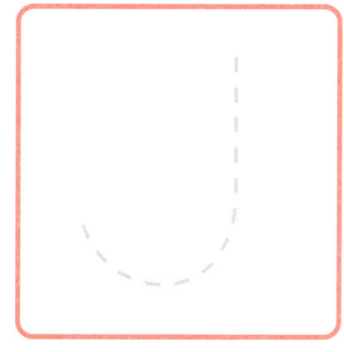
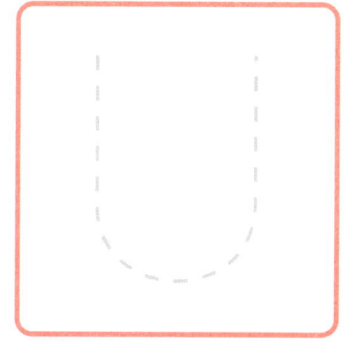

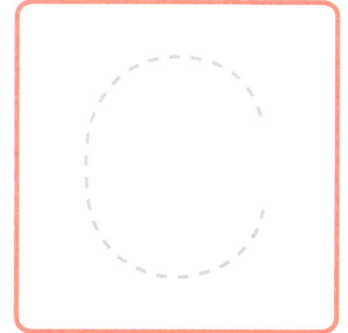
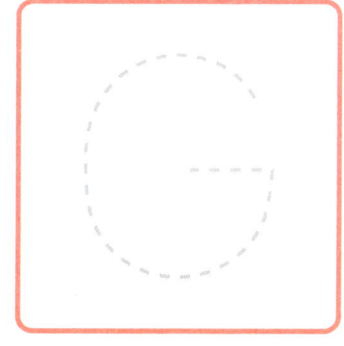
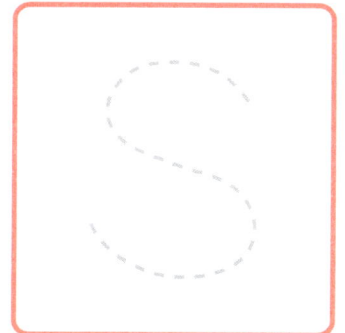

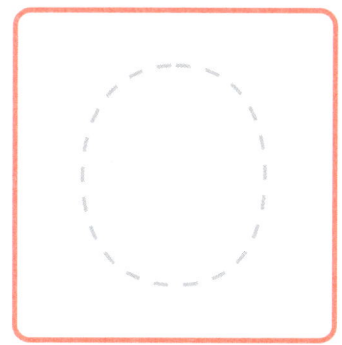
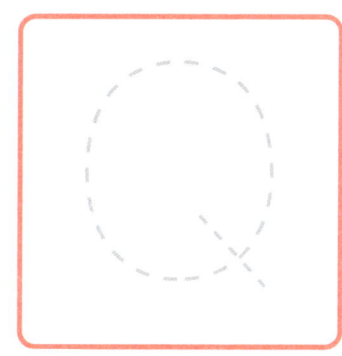

Writing A, B, and C

■ Draw a line from the dot (●) to the star (★).
Follow the order of the numbers.

A B C D E F G H I J K L M N O P Q R S T U V W X Y Z

Name

Date

■ Draw a line from the dot (●) to the star (★).
Follow the order of the numbers.

A B C **D E F** G H I J K L M N O P Q R S T U V W X Y Z

Writing G, H, and I

■ Draw a line from the dot (●) to the star (★).
  Follow the order of the numbers.

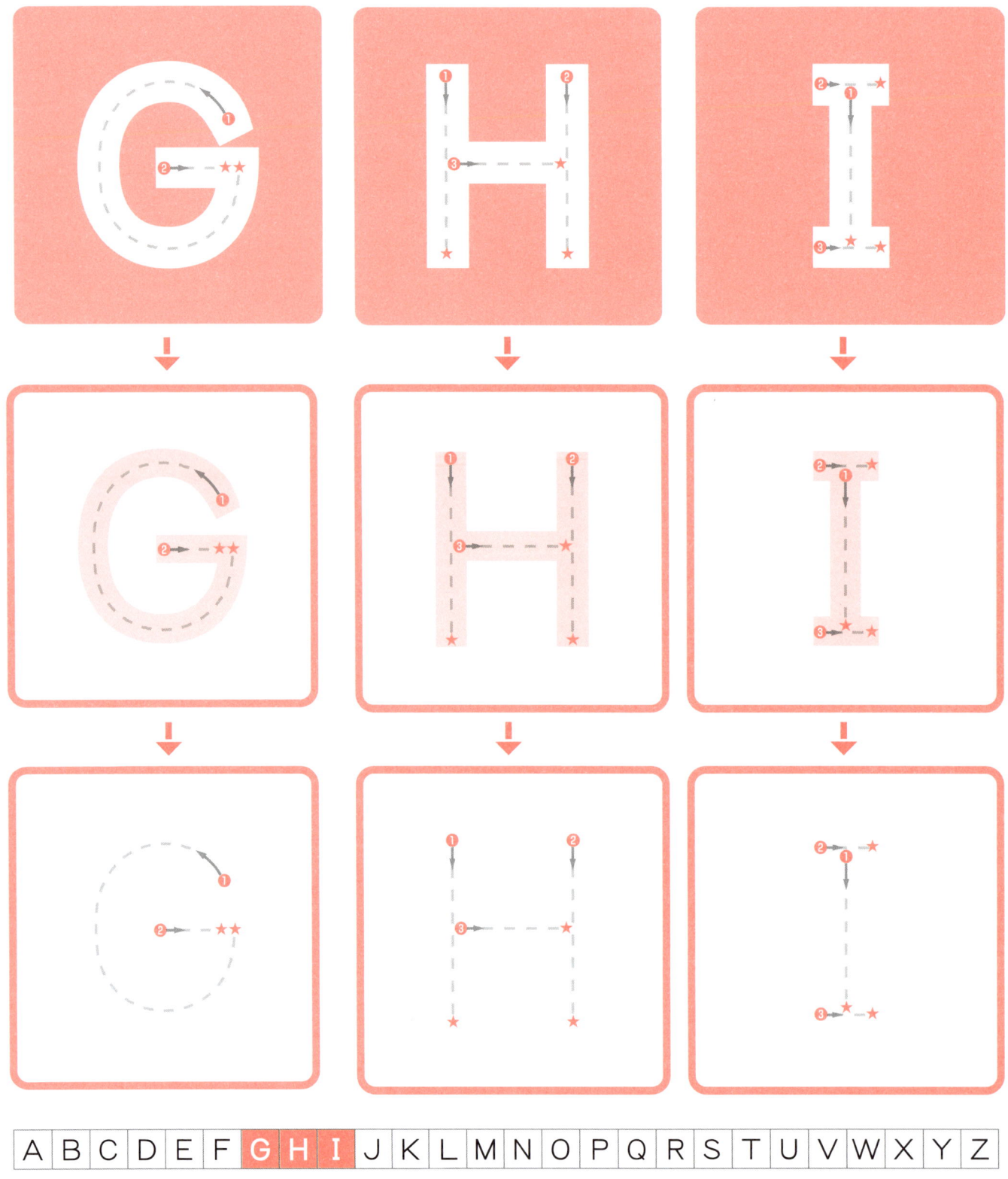

A B C D E F **G H I** J K L M N O P Q R S T U V W X Y Z

Review
Writing J, K, and L

■ Draw a line from the dot (●) to the star (★).
Follow the order of the numbers.

| A | B | C | D | E | F | G | H | I | **J** | **K** | **L** | M | N | O | P | Q | R | S | T | U | V | W | X | Y | Z |

Writing M, N, and O

■ Draw a line from the dot (●) to the star (★).
Follow the order of the numbers.

Review

Writing P, Q, and R

- Draw a line from the dot (●) to the star (★).
  Follow the order of the numbers.

| A | B | C | D | E | F | G | H | I | J | K | L | M | N | O | **P** | **Q** | **R** | S | T | U | V | W | X | Y | Z |

Writing S, T, and U

■ Draw a line from the dot (●) to the star (★).
Follow the order of the numbers.

Review

Writing V, W, and X

■ Draw a line from the dot (●) to the star (★).
  Follow the order of the numbers.

| A | B | C | D | E | F | G | H | I | J | K | L | M | N | O | P | Q | R | S | T | U | V | W | X | Y | Z |

Writing Y and Z

■ Draw a line from the dot (●) to the star (★).
Follow the order of the numbers.

| A | B | C | D | E | F | G | H | I | J | K | L | M | N | O | P | Q | R | S | T | U | V | W | X | Y | Z |

Review
Writing A-Z

Name

Date

■ Trace the letters A to Z.

A

B

C

D

E

F

G

H

I

J

K

L

M

N

O

P

Q

R

S

T

U

V

W

X

Y

Z

■ Write the letters A to Z, as shown on the left.

A

B

C

D

E

F

G

H

I

J

K

L

M

N

O

P

Q

R

S

T

U

V

W

X

Y

Z

You are now able to read and write
uppercase letters A to Z.
Congratulations!

KUM◯N

Certificate of Achievement

_____

is hereby congratulated on completing

My First Book of Uppercase Letters

Presented on _____ , 20 ____

_____
Parent or Guardian